WITHDRAWN

WORN, SOILED, OBSOLETE

Those Drinking Days

17

Books by Donald Newlove

Novels

THE PAINTER GABRIEL

SWEET ADVERSITY
embodying the author's final revisions of his
Siamese twin novels,
LEO & THEODORE
and
THE DRUNKS

ETERNAL LIFE

Life Study

THOSE DRINKING DAYS
Myself and Other Writers

In Preparation

LASERIUM
An Expedition to the Interior of the Great Memory
(Novel in three volumes)

John Berryman
William Faulkner
F. Scott Fitzgerald
Ernest Hemingway

Those

Jack London
Robert Lowell
Malcolm Lowry
J. P. Marquand
John O'Hara
Eugene O'Neill
Edwin Arlington Robinson
Theodore Roethke
Tennessee Williams
Thomas Wolfe

New York

Donald Newlove

Drinking Days

Myself

and Other

Writers

Horizon Press

Credits

Over the years some of these pages appeared in *Esquire*, *The Village Voice* and *Evergreen Review*. All are so vastly revised as to claim being new work.—D.N.

THIS ONE'S FOR YOU, MAMA

You'll have to forgive the language . . .
and a few other sins.

I want my place, my own place, my true place in the world, my proper sphere, my thing which Nature intended me to perform when she fashioned me thus awry, and which I have vainly sought all my life-time.

—Hawthorne

Contents

To the Reader

This is for my fellow writers who are still out there walking in front of cars.

Think of us at a big table, and it's evening and we're all floating on the fellowship of being writers together. Breathing, eager spirits, happy to be in this brotherhood, and willing to be moved by the perils and ironies being told over by the speaker. With luck he'll be in good form tonight.

And seated among us at the table are some of the brightest dead drunks of the century, some dear guys we've all loved who once jumped off of boats into the Caribbean or in a moment's derangement stepped out into midnight traffic or tried to leap from a plane between doctors. Or laid back and died more slowly, by the ounce. I love these writers and know that we share one talent that makes everyone at this table peers, companions in alcohol, and that is our genius for self-deceit. So when I speak of them in figuring forth this genius we share, they bless me. They know that we all breathe the same losses at this table.

And now, as Baudelaire asks, When shall we set sail for happiness? Our big table lifts. The speaker rises. He looks fit and brimming with himself. This should be a great night.

—D. N.

Part One

Drunkspeare

Dostoievsky said it: *In all things I go to the uttermost extreme.*

Good evening.

My name is Don Newlove. Sometime ago I went to the uttermost extreme, and stayed there about twenty-five years. Now I'm back. This is about writers who drank, went mad and are dead.

Each was mad in his own way and to a different depth, but each had his genius pickled by disease. Some few knew the rebirth of getting unpickled. But it takes a miracle to unpickle a genius and pluck him from his barrel of manias. All nature is against it, and so is the victim. Recovery is rare. The chances against it are staggering. It's like turning a pickle back into a cucumber. A miracle! Judging by the famous dead drunks among American writers, recovery is as rare as a martini on the moon. You have to call this a fatal disease. Alcoholism kills.

And yet . . . some few escape.

I don't care to butt heads with the dead, or to scold living drunks who write. Almost to a man these dead geniuses spoke of themselves as heavy drinkers, as did I. Masterful, self-controlled heavy drinkers. Not drunks, my God, no. At worst, and to make one's self-image truly and formally clear, the term might be "functional alcoholic." But even that terrible label has a soulful thrust to it, as if *this drunk* is completely in focus! If I can still think—just think—then I'm half-way sober and can catch those fleeting ingenuities that otherwise get by me. Feel ripe, fruitful, ready to work. Down deep I'm alive, the spirit is moving. The eye cocked for danger, though I'm just sitting at the typewriter, you know, not driving, not walking into walls or banging doorways, bureaus, table corners, chairs—I'd tell myself all my leg and arm bruises came from vitamin deficiency. Most folks don't understand the drinker. His recovery is never in doubt: after a quick facial at the cold water tap, some coffee, a shower, he's ready for more. Eager to work. All business. He relishes his fate, is ashamed at his luckiness, applauds his spirit. He is a force.

I too am an alcoholic and once sat with my number one, el supremo smile before my typewriter, toppling in place over my copy, a farsighted blur pasted to my eyeballs. I patiently uncurled the English tongue to make it speak plain but it kept tying itself into gorgeous knots I couldn't make sense of. And if the knot had a hard glow, like sunlight on snow, then I didn't care about sense. This light overrode sense, or the need for it. Light is all. This, I'd assure myself with a thankful glance toward heaven, *this* is the best prose I've ever written.

An alcoholic, yes, but I haven't had a drink in nine years. And for fourteen years I've fought the easings of alcohol, the fast vacation. Five years seemingly were in vain, but inch by inch I crossed the ocean to a new world. Night and day my brain has been undrugged for nine years. Sometimes I'd like to get away. But that passes, like change of life, and I breathe better again. The glow of clear-mindedness comes back, and there is a shine in my blood that beggars all my old drinking dreams.

Oh, I always wanted to be a drunk, and strove for that glow from earliest adolescence, but I did not want to be anything so boring as an active alcoholic. After all, drunks drink and write romantic novels with titles out of Keats or the Bible. Ecclesiastes is popular—all is fate, all is vanity. Life is a fog. A mist! And when I came out of the mist at eighty miles an hour, having crossed the highway into oncoming tractortrailers and was jouncing through a tomato patch with vines gripping the windshield and my three-year-old son flying off the seat beside me, a deep, vast, fearful shame opened bottomlessly beneath me, and left me ghastly for days—and warned. And when a breaking leg shocked me bolt upright on the subway tracks at Ninety-sixth and Broadway at four in the morning, where I'd fallen in a blackout and now lay paralyzed with a train coming at me, I knew in every cell that I was an alcoholic. Or I knew it the next morning, being told by my rotting blue leg and the big white thighbone lump lifting the skin.

Ah, then I longed for self-control, and mastery over intake. I yearned to become a social drinker. Someday! someday I'd make a mint from the movies and book clubs and take off for gracious living in Paris and Rome and Barcelona, with wine in a basket, at every meal drinking in the genteel manner of the Parisians and Romans, no longer bound to my Lower East Side daily gallon of red—but a transfigured gentleman drinker at last. This dream surged with sad, earnest desire. Call it hope, or blind prayer. I didn't know I was praying, I just felt a big ball of death under my breastbone. My selfesteem was so low that if a bar-drinker in a movie ordered bottled beer, not draft, I felt jealousy. I wanted his income and social mastery, though I took deep comfort in the pleasure of my draft, thought it less gassy and bottomlessly quaffable. I knew draft was a hard, golden, lasting joy beyond the caprices of bottled beer. I enjoyed being bottom dog.

And yet one morning I awakened to find my bedroom peopled with three corpses standing over me, their heads crushed, eyes lightless, bones warped. Horror rippled in blue waves from my soles to my charged scalp, froze me for eight unbroken hours in a bliss of fear, my heart fighting for each beat like a pigeon dying in a gutter—and I knew I was an alcoholic, beyond escaping by land or sea. I would always have to take me with me, and take that unspeakable blood-joined twin whose pickled smile said, I'll come too, buster.

But stop? What would I do on that far off belustered day when I was invited to cocktails at the Plaza with T. S. Eliot and Robert Lowell? Or to dinner and a chinning session at Norman Mailer's ropefilled jungle gym? What will I say to Papa Hemingway when he takes me into Harry's Bar in Venice for a frosted Gordon's martini in Harry's refrigerated glasses? These were deep thoughts.

Unanswerable. Decisive. I was fated to drink.

Character is alcohol.

So I lived with an overweight gorilla which only got bigger every night and day I let it out. For awhile I gave it a black Times Square cowboy hat, a redchecked Italian tablecloth shirt I let flap, frowzy blue-jean shorts, and thirty-nine-cent rubber Korean sandals, and in this costume sometimes sent it out to look for women. Always with a book, *The Brothers Karamazov* was a nice conversation piece, if my gorilla planned to do all the talking. It'd sit at the bar at the Old Stanley's or The Annex or Vajac's, trying to take in a page. But the ink was grease, the sentences self-destructed, and it kept rereading the same rubber paragraph that bulged and stretched beyond meaning. In twenty-five years of book-carrying it never brought home one woman from a bar, never picked up anything but a beer. It was too sensitive, too shy to make any kind of suggestive invitation to a girl in a bar. And something about my gorilla made the girls shy. Maybe purple sunglasses over winestained teeth.

Yesterday I had a day I couldn't buy for a million. I didn't drink. Today I have today, a Mississippi of fresh spirit flowing through me moment by moment, from my first waking second. Each morning for all those years of exhausting drinking, I promised myself a good night's rest tonight (oh, for some giant hand to come down, pick me up and carry me to bed), and after the first drink forgot all about it. A good night's rest! Simple, huh? About midnight I'd get a second wind at the typewriter and ride a red wave of vino into the city silence. About three in the morning a page snarls hopelessly. I'm all tangled ankles, haggard with wrong words. Surely five minutes rest will clear my mind, then I'll get the nits out of these snarls and go to bed. I melt into the kitchen linoleum for five minutes, planning to get up refreshed, hit that sentence and breeze off to bed. At six or seven in the morning I detach my crusted cheek from the floor and in the mirror eye my waffled new face, some dented, misshapen Dane weighing his fate. I don't see a drunk. I see a beast in the first-light. Who now, half-asleep, will shave himself bloody, shake before the dried Chinese leftovers and sour milk in his icebox, long for a last five minutes on his floor mattress, lock up his cell and slog forth to work. Rest, rest! Oh, for some tax-return windfall or elevator accident and suit for damages, to break a leg and get laid up, or jailed so that I could write in peace. Milton and Bunyan did great work in jail. Dr. Johnson says that the threat of hanging has wondrous power to clear the mind. Anything that will force me to bring peace to my cells!

You may think I never enjoyed drinking. Ha!—I was Zorba, and I had a zither named Ethyl. She made life combustible, volatile and limpid. I was Zorba the dancer, as were all these aerial beings I am about to show at their arts—and at their ruinous romance with Ethyl. Grounded angels, each at his own uttermost extreme in Little Dream-land, waiting for that healing mist to settle on his cells: inspiration that would leap from the clouded sun within. Their art burned for awhile on the forward surge of alcohol, their hearts lifted on the wink of gin, and they surfed and surfed as the wave curled over them. From the beyond they return, briefly sit here, and wish me well. They bless me as I speak. They help.

They say, *Be savage*.

My father died on a windy streetcorner in Erie.

He died of tuberculosis, diabetes and alcohol. Diabetics should not drink. Out of the county hospital two days, he stopped into a poolroom for a couple of stiffeners and a game of eight-ball. One drink joined the next as his adrenals and pancreas jolted out the high and we buried him. The threat of death to a drunk? Peanuts.

He died of alcohol as surely as did three close friends I tried to help stay sober. My poet-novelist friend Gil fell dead on the street and was buried by the city on Hart's Island. My pianist friend Roy, once a Gurdjieff dancer, overdosed for the third time in a year—this time wine on pills—and was picked up stiff on his fire escape and shipped home to Atlanta in a box. My rich architect friend Alexander, a giant on his last legs, drank a thirty-nine-cent pint of rubbing alcohol in his well-stocked toolroom-workshop overlooking the Hudson, and convulsed to death on the hardwood from which I'd dragged him to bed. I'd poured his booze down the sink. Next morning he woke up and drank isopropyl. After seventeen trips to the wards, he thought he was stronger than isopropyl. He had a gusto for hospitals. A tank corps massed against his first drink would have been laughed aside. He'd wake up gray as death and if he couldn't finger the dial for the grog shop, he'd drink anything. He thought good work came from perfect loneliness and was worth any price. He was a two-fisted perfectionist. No matter that his thirst for it drove his wife from their home, and iced all human feeling, leaving him shut up with his tools. Ask him about losses or suggest that holding back from drink might help lift his loneliness, he'd brush that stuff aside: "I'm looking for a nymphomaniac who owns a bar!" This was bluff. He could have bought a bar and would have been useless to a nymphomaniac. In the wards he trained on mouthwash and hair tonics. He was a damaged man, his big grey eyes were blitzed, and he jittered. The wood alcohol in his toolroom was a last resort. I don't know how often he was driven to it, but he thought he could handle it even if it wasn't his drug of choice.

Isopropryl is the chief solvent in antifreeze and shrivels brain cells. He may not have been in his right mind that last time he drank it, or been in delirium. Who can say? Nobody was there. He was perfectly alone.

As John Donne says, Rather dead than change.

But this is not a lecture, except to myself. I no longer pour booze down the sink. The drunk must do that or it's meaningless, if not dangerous with someone as far-gone as Alex. I was new at the time. But I worked hard with these guys, made many hospital calls as they sat around in their paper slippers, brought books and cigarettes and some hope that they had each hit bottom at last. The third hospital I visited Roy at, I told him, "This elevator doesn't go down any farther, Roy. You're gonna have to get off." He sighed. "You're right, Don. I feel this is it at last." But we were both mistaken. He was a Georgian and one summer night soon after, he bought some of the sweet strawberry wine he loved, and some packages of "perfectly legal drugs from the drugstore that anybody can buy, Don," and took his mattress onto his fire escape and—blindly, perhaps—ended his drinking days, still the lonely and softspoken sweettalker who conned himself with sunbeams about the joy of walking through Central Park stoned. He'd walked into a subway stanchion years earlier and lost his two front teeth. They were still missing when he died. I memorialized them, in a way, by granting his gap-toothed smile to my Siamese twin Teddy in *Sweet Adversity*.

I'd rather be dead than live over that life of raging good cheer I once granted myself, not knowing I was ill. I too once hovered on that bottomless bottom that sucked away Alex and Roy (more on Gil later) and wore the same mask of reason and honesty that killed them. I tried to help them lift the fingers of mist from their brains, and was moved by their deaths—but reservedly moved. I feel most booze deaths come about by self-deceit, an injustice to ourselves so deep that we are supersensitive to all our lesser flaws, and forever fear we have insulted, failed, injured or wronged others as viciously as we've

17

wronged ourselves; I was "terribly sorry" about some universal act of unkindness on my part and asked your forgiveness for my every thought or gesture. I could still reason, but in some deeper place I lived in a stupor of guilt. I feared being spied upon, hid titles of books I carried, and harassed myself to give off a look of fearless honesty—I was sick with policing myself and during unguarded moments would spot a disappointed hound in my eyes. Well, we were all sick dogs in a fog of guilts. But even though some of us finally got honest with ourselves, that eternally sniffing bloodhound doesn't go away. I can smell booze and guilt through a brick wall—it's a curse. So, when a sick friend dies after years of many different helping hands, it's hard to feel tragic. About a man who lied to himself with great firmness, albeit in a mist? Why sentimentalize dishonesty? Better, much better to think twice about this disease. Very few of us get out of the mist. So few it's breathtaking, and I ask, Why me, why this unutterable luck?

When Dad died I wasn't told until the next day. I hadn't seen him in a year or so. My sister phoned the night he died, but my wife took the call and I was so out of it that she decided to wait until the next day to tell me. As we drove in from the country with my drinking hearties, my wife told me from the back seat, "Don, I have bad news for you. Your father died yesterday. I couldn't tell you last night, you were having such a good time." My fellow writers were quiet. The best I could do at last was quote *Gatsby*: "The poor sonofabitch." But I was soon milling his death into the stuff of verse, alone with paper and broadnib and two quarts of my favorite heavy sherry. Could I really come up with some lines to match those burning memorialists, Jonson and Sidney? Drinker, shoot high.

Well, I boiled his bones and got jelly. I was twenty-eight and couldn't weep, knowing him mostly by banter, and my lockstep sonnet bemoaned "the alcohol, the music and the verse consuming me." I passionately meant to slip this verse next to his heart when no one was looking. But, woozy and embarrassed, a half-pint of Courvoisier in my breast pocket, I feared to weaken my atheist grip on life with tears, and was stoical at the funeral home but too sensitive to handle his jacket openly during the viewing, so it wasn't until after the ride out to the old Ripley graveyard near Lake Erie, and after the last words in windy sunlight, the sealed box fully lowered, that I lurched from my camp chair and hurled the folded epitaph down the hole as the first dirt rattled on the lid. I gasped back to my chair, blushing and charged. I'd done my best with those plaints to my father. Steel rang as I nailed the dead drunk for cheating me of my life. I sat shaking but confirmed as a writer, a harsh, gritty Tolstoy under the flapping canvas. Real life at last and I had the large mind and pitiless heart to match it. The flowers stank death and poetry. What cognac, what cognac.

So my father dies and I shoosh down sherry and drain the last elbow of brandy and set flight to my death-lyrics, or croakings. But why be so hard on that young mist-swimmer? Well, because his ghost still lives, I get hard whiffs of those old feelings, the amber moments in sherry, the allure of release like woodsmoke in my veins. My Drunkspeare stops me on the street, his fixed grin saying, One last drink, Don, one last one. Remember the lift that made your knees weak? And then the ghost of chemical ego offers some gigantic destiny in the clouds which I deserve but have been denied. He will bring down the wild goose of the perfect four-liner and hand it to me on the west wind. I am the April drunk, I bubble with old moods, under grey skies the first roses droop and burn. My eyes mist. A drink, to lock into this mood, stay fixed. My mouth pools, greedy for chemical hope, the old tastes of malt and hops, the popped cork and sniff that pierces. My Drunkspeare wants his body back to smell and taste with. And say some tidal frustration, a really baffling defeat, pricks on exactly the right nerve and hairpins into a drink? With the first breath of bourbon, Drunkspeare rushes up my nose and is home. That unholy ghost is back, ready to spur me to brilliance. No squawking, he tells me, this will be good for you. And I agree. It's so good. Why fight? Let go and enjoy yourself. And after a few ounces, the old tunes wake up, that grandeur of jingling anguish, the lick and shimmer of language, the heartbreak at the core of things. But I breathe purposefully, and well with clear energies. Aerial, I settle down, ready for the hard joys of writing, the kick down the playing field. Follow the ball, Don, I warn myself, let's not be excessive. But within two sentences my spirit sways and aches, and I am borne downriver on buoyancy and pain. I strive to breathe each phrase. Each syllable has its germ of light. Sentences eddy with insights, then swerve dangerously, but I follow ths sparks. What a rhythm I'm into! Let it build, don't look back. A paragraph swells. I burst with bliss and yet am all nerves that it won't come out right. I keep at it but now the stream bends. Where did that thought go I was following? Is it lost? I try to force it back with a slap and pinch my nose. As I head for the cold water tap for a facial, I turn to stone, the thought leaps into my mouth and I rush to my desk. The keys jam. But I get it down and sit back. Does it really follow the sentence before? The day darkens. A right verb dies, flattened by a moved comma. Some filigree melts. A cadence falls short of the beat. Now I write despite fading buoyancy, turn on the lamps, study the page-glare. Look back. My lift drains. Here is a cold Latin root I want Englished, always rewarding dictionary work, but I'm tired. Still looking back, I go stale. This is it, I'm stuck at retightening unsprung sentences if I want this paragraph tuned like a Rolls. Something chokes and suddenly I'm all over the page fighting breakdowns. Heartfelt words seize up. I go to clipboard and move to my rocker. Soon, false starts entwine the margins, inserts bear inserts, words crawl everywhere and curl up-sidedown over the top, phrases hang from spidery lines leading up and down into smudge. And I sense massive gaps ahead. Time for a refill! Now I scrape harshly but racing thoughts spurt uncurbed, the page smears, similes mismatch, the big spark dulls. I loll in my chair, shout at myself for strength. Sit back for the big overview of a hairline crack leading to a meddlesome speck so stupid I'm breathless. The work it means! But I sit at my desk once more, typing myself dry, wringing my spirit stiff, and even after that go on, fibers parched, brain glaring, gambling on ingenuity, ghost-weaving into the night.

My trunk is stuffed to the lid with dead novels in manuscript, wine dreams that became forced marches, each more painful to write than the last—or more chemically joyous. A mania for originality gripped me and the cost was clear before I began each book: it would be unpublishable. This was still possible in the Fifties and early Sixties, even necessary—to keep style sacred. Avoid the gray grist of the undead, the moneymakers at their grinding. A breakthrough will come. But I need strength to keep originality alive. Much sacrifice, too. Nothing and no one can become so dear that I waver and sell out. I need a heavy mist of originality to veil my shortcomings, a very rich voice for my flights. Let each sentence gleam deep as amber, glow green as a horsefly, shine like nicked lead. Wash grandly with Shakespearean bliss, over big clumps of large and meaningful pauses, toward Promethean periods. World conquerors must be fearless. And genius helps. My worst flaw: I had no genius, or gift for ideas, only grimness and a need to give my life meaning through the glory of words. Even worse for a writer, I had no power to invent stories, just desire and heartache, and strained to boost endings hovering on a catsmile. Boy, I admired Keats and Thomas Wolfe, I mean urgently. Their burnings and overflowings could help me hide my dumb endings. I felt stupid, never on top of my story, driven to blinding originality and making speech do the work of plot. So I sipped beer and worked at my flower arrangements out of Keats and Wolfe, not knowing my stories lacked spine and focus, trusting in heartbreak.

All my set-pieces were Turner sunsets. I believed in divine sensibilities. Let readers say, He writes like an angel!

My mother married four alcoholics, each of whom indirectly died of drink. They were all "drinking people," she said, meaning people who savored life and had good manners, so I come from a drinking background. Each of her husbands was a ham-fisted, wretched boor when drinking. Biff, thud . . . She still has a chin scar where my father kicked her while she was suckling me. He was a Lake Erie country boy who became a rather rakish city slicker, did factory work at General Electric and cooked for a train crew on the Nickel Plate Line, dabbled in eight-ball and the nags and drank his paycheck dry. He beat her. She was fifteen or sixteen when they married, and was glad to escape her father's horsewhip. One of her earliest memories is of being whipped to earth in the barnyard. Her dad later had a midlife conversion and became a nondrinker. He had a hard, rosy, full-bodied smile in his last years and I liked him a lot. But she escaped into city folks, who partied a great deal and used mixers with their drinks. She was beautiful and sought after and at five I thought her a ringer for Claudette Colbert whom I'd seen in a milk bath in DeMille's *The Sign of the Cross*, and in *Cleopatra*. The same heartshaped face, plucked eyebrows, wounded laugh and a touch of the queen. Biff, thud.

My earliest memory is of my first sight of alcohol, at a country bar on Lake Erie. I was four and my father had taken me out to the nightline while he fished for sturgeon. He gaffed one I thought a whale and boated it, then rowed for shore, a red railroad lamp burning on the bow. We went up to the State Line Bar. He sat me on a stool, ordered a shot, then dipped a burning kitchen match into it. The flaming matchhead seemed to go right to the heart of the shot. He raised the match out still burning, a blue flame dancing on the booze, and drank the shot. Talk about magic . . . And when I was five, I began going to movies alone and later acting out everything about alcohol I saw on the screen, the magic change it worked on suave, stagy actors in evening clothes. I knew about redeye before I could spell my name.

My first stepfather was a bloated, purplelipped Hitler who ruled a huge German drinking-hall in Erie and was violent. My mother and older sister and I moved into our first house together and were soon terrorized speechless by this monster of rant. Mother soothed us at bedtime with talks about our good luck. "Hang on, my young ones, better days are coming!" What came was Christmas morning and crazed with hangover he threw my sister June through a glass cocktail table, belted Mama's eye, and heaved the ripped out Christmas tree off the front porch. This biliousness eventually burst his spleen and he died within a year. He'd been a charmer our first months together, full of alcoholic gladhanding, and we dressed nicely for show at his hall. But his will left us flat. We moved into a matchbox and Mama found work as a hatcheck girl. He was not missed. But I still see his bearlipped joy over wurst and beer, his half-lidded, popeyed guzzler's glow. The shine of his cunning. And I think twice about this tyrant who burst and died at my very age as I write this. I hate the illness but not the man; his kindness once entranced my mother.

My second stepfather, crazed Irishman whose staggering Catholic guilts had whitened his hair while still young, owned a much fancier club and kept a fully stocked wine cellar at home. He opened his restaurant the day after Prohibition died, that flawed battle against grief and plague. He too was violent and more than once as a boy I jumped on his back and ripped out white hair by the fistsful. He tried to ship me out of sight to The Manlius School, where I was a sixteen-year-old cadet, but after my first year a bad-conduct letter was sent saying I could not return. I dizzied with embarrassment when he read me this during a livingroom court-martial (he'd had an ex-Secretary of State, an admired friend, write my commendation for entrance). I'd failed flat, and my sins enlarged under his alcoholic perfectionism, his old-soldier sentiments as a doughboy who'd fought the Kaiser, and I'd undercut his trials with his priests—he would not marry my non-Catholic mother and lived in mortal sin, foreseeing hell vividly (his drinker dad had died in a madhouse) while trying to save face by sending my sister to a Catholic girls school and me to Manlius. Being drummed out was no loss to me; I did not fit in and was not liked at military school; but today I remember the physical rhapsody of the grounds, the stifled ardor of my body in spring, boogie-woogie and cadging butts in the game room when the smoking lamp was lit. And my worries about Mama facing him alone each night.

He saved every issue of *Esquire*, the glossy men's magazine which tied alcohol with clothing. He bought all his fabrics six months before they appeared in this bible—the first box plaid suit in town (no waist!), a yellow cashmere coat that matched his ego. He stocked every booze advertised in its pages, loved gabbing about the New York bistros, waving his hand familiarly and snickering over nights on the town. His small-town soul was soaked in Manhattan's alcohol culture and he snobbed on the magazine's highhandedness. (That forty years later I was to be a featured writer and listed in its masthead as a contributing editor would have been beyond belief.) I am literally a child of *Esquire*, or hidden sin of Mr. Esky's, since my first drinks wers stolen bottles of Tanqueray, Beefeater, Cutty Sark, Lemon Hart Jamaica, molassesdark Myers, Benedictine, Drambuie, Cointreau, Triple Sec, Hennessy, Courvoisier, Grand Marnier, that orangeblossom Scotch liqueur, Hudson Bay hundred-and-fifty-one proof, and the wines, aperitifs, akvavits—please don't leave, I'll be through in a moment—and all the exotic glassware, the small clear cordial glass, the smooth urn of a doubleshot glass with a fine red ring around it, the heavy cutbottom glass for something harsh and straight on the rocks, the champagne standup bra-cup, the deep brilliant bulb of the afterdinner snifter, the longstemmed martini, the manhattan brimmer, the toddy cup, the stein—forget chemistry sets, these were the toys of my late boyhood, and at thirteen I was smoking my stepfather's kingsize silken filtertips with the logo of a Britisher in tophat, monocle and cane. On my bedroom dresser rose a tall frosted Zombie glass with its decal of a Haitian witchdoctor—*No More Than Two*! That magazine—it came poached in vermouth. I had my little white statuette of Old Grand-Dad with his doped

pinpoint eyes and drained grin wrinkling with constipation. I
wore three white shirts daily, French cuff, turquoise studs,
knew my wines and Havanas, doted on heavy Southern
Comfort hundred-proof which was liquid honeysuckle, and my
mother had a display cabinet in the dining room loaded with
every miniature in the world of grog. I stole creme de menthe,
creme de cacao, strawberry liqueur, banana, some goldflaked
brandy or amber gin, peach nectar, apricot, raspberry,
blackberry, anise, and in the great new pink refrigerator
commanding our kitchen were Heineken's, Miller's,
Michelob, Guinness stout, and knockout Black Horse Ale from
Canada for real punch. I saved little plastic Black and White
Scotties, Carstairs seals with medicine balls, Vat 69 ashtrays,
fancy swizzlesticks, pousse caffe novelty glasses, and we had a
rolling mahogany liquor wagon in the livingroom, with ice
bucket and siphon and seltzer bombs. My stepfather wore a
silkstitched midnight blue smoking jacket to drink in when
company came and it was great, and it was just windowdressing
on booze, the wagon, the jacket, and all the hops and malts and
flavorings, just little bow ties on alcohol.

I'd tongue the last drop from one of Mama's little
blackberry or banana miniatures in the wash room between
classes. Going in as an A student, I failed ninth grade (I'd
repeated first because of illness)—but I blamed this on the
numbing effect of my morning cigarettes. This new failure so
flattened me, being class vice president, that I joined the
Marines. I hoped to find manliness and *esprit de corps*. Sex,
too. I found myself in the same bay with Guadalcanal veterans,
survivors of Iwo Jima and Saipan beachheads, who lovingly and
with deep thought nicknamed me "Precious." At seventeen
Precious was a hard name to live with among men who just had
been out lobbing grenades in earnest and machine-gunning
and bayonetting Japanese, men with white wild eyes and
nicknames like Wardog and sporting hard purple wounds like
medals. Nightly they'd sprawl dead drunk and stark naked on
their blankets, fearless of dawn hardons. I was already a

serviceable beerdrinker, despite my priceless standing in the bay, blacking out and vomiting regularly so I could drink more, and in one blackout during a payday poker game over locker-boxes, I bet a ruby ring I'd had for two years and was amazed next day to see an old Iwo vet wearing it. I asked and he told me bluntly I'd bet and lost it. That was the first valued article I was to lose in a blackout, and it was like having a psychic finger chopped off.

Blackouts weren't new. In Jamestown, my small South-western New York hometown, they'd begun for me at fifteen when I'd had my birth certificate copied and set in plastic, after doctoring the date with lemon juice, a trick I'd learned not two years earlier from my invisible ink kit when I was The Shadow and roaming Jamestown's midnight yards. My new adult costume was a banker's black homburg and charcoal pinstripe with vest, and I'd grown a moviestar mustache and could step up to any bar, usually without being asked my age. I always broke bills down into ones, flashed the fat billfold of a heavy tipper, and drank quietly, eyes crimped and wounded by lost love. Even at fifteen, when I went out into the bar world, my only beer-limit was money, and already I had the knack of puking, soaking and recombing my hair, and of springing out of the men's room with eager step. I rarely knew I was drunk and would tank up to the very top before going home. I stopped only when no more would go in (ha ha ha!) or the bar closed or my wallet gave off a death-cough. Then gaps started appearing in my nights. I blacked out early one evening about nine, and woke up next morning in bed with a Zulu spear through my brain and eyes like carpets the wine has dried in. Were these blood clots my eyes? Where'd I go, what'd I do? My brain feels black and blue. I search for head lumps. Hard stuff! I must have switched, nothing else possible. This loss was something longer than my flickering greyouts where I'd lose an hour or so of bar chat or come out of it on the wrong bus or standing under silent elms on a strangely brilliant streetcorner. This morning there was nothing, only flashings of early evening, happy beers—and blotto. I stopped by the fountain where I worked and asked my fellow sodajerks, had they seen me, did I stop by? No. But it was clear enough: blackouts were a commonplace (so common they had no name), a drinker's burden, and a lost hour here and there was not too harsh a price, and could be weirdly amusing. I hadn't been thinking last night. Won't happen again.

But now I wore the starched khaki pisscutter of the Marine and struck out nightly for the base slopchute and was taught man-size drinking. North Carolina's 3.2 green beers are so weak you have to slop down a case to get even half-smashed, and a case was $2.40. Each gyrene would get his case at the bar, open his throat like a rainpipe and, without swallowing, empty a bottle straight into his stomach. We'd get twenty-four swigs per case. The Marines may still drink that way at Camp Lejeune. Stagger back to my bay, lie on my back with a case in my belly, my sack swaying like a crow's nest on heavy seas, beer within slopping side to side however I rolled.

One summershot Saturday I took off for Asheville, picked up a fat girl I'd dated from a base dance Louis Armstrong blew at, and took her canoeing. My first canoe ride. There were many canoers on the lake but only I had a bag of beer and a trumpet. We paddled off into some little swamp islands. This was what I'd joined the Corps for! Alone, I found her riveted into a gigantic stiff girdle. We grappled and sweat. The canoe floated out into the lake. So eager—(shaking)—for my break-through as a stud. She pushed back bashfully as I groped about her sausage casing, then suddenly our slippery little ship flipped bottoms up. The beer sank, I spotted that first. She had her arms over the wood bottom and clutched her glasses. I thought I'd lost my trumpet but when I righted the canoe it bobbed up in its case. Boy, I was thankful. Later that night, still hoping despite the starchless disgrace of my khakis, I took her to a barn dance. Her ex-boyfriend was home from the army and he and a swabby and a third man jumped me outside the barn. Marines are famed for leather dress belts with heavy buckles they wrap aroung their fists in bar brawls. Mine was back at the base. I warned them anyway, "You guys watch out, I'm trained to kill." This didn't bother them. I went back that night with loose teeth, cracked ribs, and head so kicked and puffed I couldn't see my ear in the mirror; I swelled lopsidedly, one eye so tightshut the lashes were buried. When I'd been down and taking their boots, I turned off the pain and I remember the starry Carolina night rivering over me like Coca-Cola.

I never linked that beating with alcohol. My beery Marine egoism had faith it could take on three dogfaces and swabbies. I had only to let out a bloodcurdling cry and wade in. That's how it was back in the bay when Wardog talked about his bar fights in Asheville. And he had a Rebel yell that whitened your spine. Just a little guy, five-one or so, weighing one-forty, tops, with several welts of scar tissue, a swish dressmaker's mustache and boiling blue eyes that brimmed insanity and manliness and esprit. A thing of glory in his pressed, salt-pale fatigues, he was born staggering. Drank, that man did, a stockade hound whose steel grip on loneliness radiated self-destruction. Drink enough, maybe I could be like him. No, a sea of alcohol couldn't do that. I was still Precious, not a regular but a short-termer who would be let out now that the war had ended. He was shipping over, in a year should make corporal again. He saw no hope for me.

Living through the Marines was a great experience, like a thirteen-month childbirth, and ennobled my drinker's self-image. I thought my top sergeant a hell-master, and he was. Reporting to his orderly room for anything was to ropewalk a chasm, and my bones shook, since his military specialty was nitpicking, redfaced anger. At his glance I jumped and shouted my rank, name and reason for despoiling his eyesight. After the blood-gush he could bring to the brain, my stepfather held no further terrors for me. Even stateside, the top was saving lives under fire and practicing on me. But out I got at last, ready to weep with joy, my head for beer greatly enlarged. One noon toward the end I was pulling bay orderly when an old sodajerk hero from Jamestown flew in from Cherry Point to surprise me. Wayne was a corporal already, had fought through the South Pacific and loved tales about "the old Corps" he'd joined two years earlier. My duty ended, we went into Asheville, bought two fifths of lacerating corn popskull and a case of green beer and pooped out under a big steel bridge. This was about two in the afternoon and next I knew I was hanging over my sack puking onto the Sunday papers. To the last image, our whole afternoon and night had faded. This was the most astounding blackout so far, going from sunlight to puke with a twenty-hour gap. When I saw Wayne next he beat my back and lauded our work. "We drank everything, old buddy, not a drop wasted." My disgust on waking to puke was lifted to white heat by fear of displeasing old salts in the bay—hounds for cleanliness and spit-polished deck—and I raced for a bucket and swab, not even grabbing a waist towel, staggering, brained, bile-tongued, dried stiff as burnt bacon with the miseries of corn.

The Corps was not all horror and overcast. I warmed to two or three of my mates, stiff-set Parris Island shitbirds who had risen from bald-headed boot to full private and here at Lejeune were bucking for the glory-stripe of private first class. My Southern friends weren't mad crackers, had a touch of education and drank little. One suave music-lover hooked me with his reverence for Duke Ellington's mood pieces; I was a trumpet fan but never thought you could *love* popular music; this was uplifting. A tall, softspoken master sergeant who was my top noncom at the base exchange warehouse had a warm smile, was studying to be a thirty-third degree Mason, and took a bunch of us out to the shore, with chicken and barrels of beer, and I swam in salt water for the first time, big curling Carolina breakers, a grand day: he drank little, if at all. I passed out with longing for women. Smitty, a lofty, catsmiling Marine from Asheville, got me reading Thomas Wolfe's *You Can't Go Home Again* and Wolfe renewed my desire to be a writer. As I saw it, novelists were independently wealthy world-travelers and had sex the way I drank beers. It looked good.

I'd begun writing long heroic fantasies when I was twelve, and back home after discharge, I holed up under a bare bulb in our garage and started typing a rainwashed mystery novel highlighting Jamestown, something black and lush and post-war. But writing even a mystery was like breaking boulders—it was hard work to think clearly. Half-way, I lost heart for my mystery, whose plot cramped my Wolfean ardor, nor could I rise to the bitter grey writerliness of Chandler; so I had my first big abandoned work and took up lyrical fantasy and short stories. After a year or so, and revisions past belief, my first story collection, *The Green and the Gray*, bounced at Scribner's. I didn't finish another book for eleven years, but kept at it with great heart, peppering my spirit with rejection slips, seeking a tone of deep song, some billow of language to go against the numb grey journalizing of the realists being published. Kept at it, kept at it, and slipped daily into a long death. I never knew I was dying.

Hate the realists I did but my overcast deepened and brought out a rich grey glare I fought against but that lapped my heart. It would not go away. I thought overcast my natural state. Grey days were my meat. My idea of sublime verse was Swinburne's line about Villon:

Bird of the bitter bright gray golden morn

Sweet agony! I savored Shakespearean black, "death's dateless night" and "to the edge of doom" and Macbeth's murk, Hamlet's graveyard glories, Lear's swoop of night—these were the human spirit's highwatermarks. I drank up Céline's *Journey to the End of the Night*, the black rant of *Death on the Installment Plan*. I sucked at my Eliot, and agreed with Keats—

> *I have been half in love with easeful Death,*
> *Called him soft names in many a mused rhyme,*
> *To take into the air my quiet breath;*
> *Now more than ever seems it rich to die,*
> *To cease upon the midnight with no pain. . .*

I cherished (and still do) Dostoievsky's huge rainy night-piece at the heart of *The Possessed*. I sought touchstones of darkness. My twenties were a deep soak in radiant depression.

This was not a savage, galvanic despair favored by Wolfe. I lacked his genius for gloom. Mine was steady chemical overcast that made the day gritty and breath short. My writer's honesty demanded that I think twice about the streets I lived on in Jamestown, see through our great elms, the avenues of air and daylight, and face the cinders everywhere underfoot. One winter night my sister June's baby strangled in his crib. The grave was living rock, or so it felt, with first snow feathering us. I was reading *Dubliners* at the time and Joyce too was living rock, shading lives from city stone, then shaping them into snowflakes falling into the dark Shannon. The dead baby was heavier than all the books in the great stone fort of the James Prendergast Free Library, and another midnight touchstone for the just eye to weigh with.

I was the sanest man on earth, saw all with bleaching clearness and, living on adrenalin and irony, had to fight to smile: all my jokes were deadly, "I love it" meant "I hate it"—I said nothing straight out, only through a sieve of irony. Even sober, it was chemical irony, forced good cheer despiting "hell under the breastbone," as Whitman says. My fellowship of sodajerks, once bonded by beer, petered out into poker games and died. Warehouse inventories in the Corps had disciplined me for forced marches on the typewriter. I'd met my first wife-to-be and was less sex-starved. Not less love-starved. I was not giving away any part of me I needed for writing, and what love I had was locked into my ego and spent on soul-fulfilling word flights. Once recognized and independently wealthy, perhaps I would feel free to bestow love. I short-changed everyone to save my strength. The burning page was my defense against the clear logic of suicide. Oh, I thought I loved, her if anyone, but what was heaven itself was the gush of sex and that could be had with equal intensity from any woman. It didn't come from the woman anyway, it came from me. I saw . . . and knew I did not have to commit my heart to anyone. I needed my heart! Saying I love you in a voice that I believed could not be done, so I tried rarely, and then lied. I was full of formal lies. Once the force of sex spent itself my mind moved magnetically to the typewriter, and I couldn't wait to get away unless more sex was to be wrung from her. I went to her family dinners, my best suit and good manners mere masks of lust. She knew it!—and lighted into me with long kitchensink arias. How I strained to work up an honest I love you—but my writer's honesty, and absolute focus on self, made every word grate in my throat. Wisely, she never convinced herself I meant it. I'd met my match in honesty and it was steel against steel. My ego had many strengths, as an ex-Marine, a writer and poet (and poseur and shameless thief of ideas), a quick eye in an honest face, a surging urgency to make great works (never, never to write journalism or dim my high seriousness with any humor less than solemn irony), and so on, and not one of these could overpower her wit. I got what I gave. "I don't love you, Don," she'd tell me, even after I'd chased her about New York State for three years. Earnest vows and long soupy arguments round the clock, nothing moved her. "It's my birthday today. Did you bring me flowers? Never mind a gift, just some flowers. Or did you plan to give me two bunches next year?" "Kill me, I deserve to die." I could admit to any fault, and did, to my regret, but not to that one weakness which shielded my greatest strength: alcoholic egoism. I didn't know I was a drunk.

How could this escape my notice? It did. Of all possible insights into myself, as petty storethief, egomaniac fearful of appearances, or intellectual snob, this was the least likely and would have struck at my most costly and conscious trust with myself: that I was honest. Honest to the hilt, unsparing of every known flaw in my character, and I'd parade them before her, but not that. It was too close for both of us to see. There must be some larger meaning behind these mysterious failings she found so unfailingly in me and I never failed to show. Were I to bring flowers without being thrice warned of the nearing birthday, it would be out of sheer cunning, as a bedwarmer, a gift paired with a choice wine for oiling the bedsprings. Anything to dim that light she turned on me. All hearts and flowers had my greasy happiness as goal. I thought our differences were biological, that our fights were for life and would arise with any woman I married. That I wore a mask of reason to cover my chemically overblown self-importance as a man of words, and that my flaws had at their core no greater mysterious source, I could not grant. It would have meant changing.

The chase changed course when I was recalled to the Marines for Korean service, ran down to the post office and joined the Air Force to avoid those Near Eastern beachheads awaiting my old wardog buddies. Four more years!—the shortest tour I could enlist for in the Air Force. But I'd get out alive, maybe with a Wolfe-sized war novel already researched. I'd lost all desire for esprit, esprit turned my stomach, I was a writer-loner and eager to live and drink another day. She was going to Barnard when I came to see her after a year of stateside travels, then a year on Long Island and transfer to New Jersey, and I arrived in uniform, my new age wearing a look of piercing Olympian realism, and biting lip to match, both enriched by beer, and begged her unmercifully to marry me. I got what I gave. She still didn't love me. But she was aging, now twenty-three, as much atheist as I, and perhaps marriage would lend a sanctity to life that the God I'd ripped from her years earlier had left empty. She was superhumanly busy, a language student racing about to ignore her losses; maybe peace was possible; there'd be more money married; and swearing vows was an adventure. I think she loved me before I loved her. She was forgiving, less biting. She enjoyed making meals on my weekends free from the base, and sitting with wine and candles over fish and an Italian salad. Like John O'Hara, I had a rage to live and this tiny apartment was a fresh start with shining floor and clean sheets. So small the rooms. I felt my weight wherever I moved. To sit in a chair with a bar of early Saturday afternoon sunlight on the plants was hope. About a year after we married we were at table and I poured the wine and sat back waiting while she broke the French loaf, and her gesture of breaking bread in candlelight struck me with her mortality. I sat cloven with love.

A few months later she was pregnant, a surprise, and we moved to New Egypt, New Jersey, a tiny village near my Air Force base, and she had our son Stuart Ernest at the base hospital. He was middlenamed Ernest in memory of Hemingway who was reported to have died the day before in a plane crash in Africa. I was stirred and on the brink of serious mourning should the papers confirm his death. No—obits were appearing and I was over the brink. My wife was in the hospital when I got a call at the NCO club that she was in labor. When I reached the delivery room my son lay alone in a room apart, born just five minutes earlier, still bare and purple, ruby blood in his navel rocking as he bawled. After half an hour I was allowed to see my wife for the first time since driving her to the hospital. She'd been shaking in bed for three days under a mound of blankets. The hospital wouldn't admit her early. She demanded that I insist and I fought back. Now her lips had a serene sheen as she came out of anesthesia, and she smiled wordlessly, then with a hint of delight lifted herself up a bit, looking both ways at bedstands beside her.

"Where are they?" she whispered, her skin silken with release.

"What are you looking for?"

"My flowers." Her mouth trembled. "All of the wives have flowers, Don."

"I had to race to get here, Sweetie."

She broke into tears and turned her face away.

Next day I brought roses. But her milk had soured overnight and she could not breastfeed. She never did, and blamed me. She was blackly thoughtful for months whenever heating a bottle. She looked hard-punched but ready for rounds two through fifteen. I was joyous and celebrating my hero's thick skin. Hemingway had walked out of the jungle, the papers said, with a bunch of bananas and two fifths of Gordon's gin in his arms. "My luck," he told newsmen, "she is still good." I partook of his luck and felt deathproof. Let her be blue. I'm a rhino about self-pity in women.

Some months later, sitting with an untaxed beer in the club, I read Faulkner's Nobel Prize speech in the *Times* with a back-prickle, a catch in my throat, and red mist on my eyes. He'd gotten the prize for *A Fable* (in the afterglow of finishing it, he'd foolishly told reporters that it was the best novel of his times and rivaled in this century of American novels only by Thomas Wolfe's daring to grasp the ungraspable), and for his life's work, and I'd admired the liquid poetic effects of *A Fable*, if not the tearful grandeur of its ending. So I thrilled and saw the heavens flare over Sweden as his world-speech dared reach for its enormous climactic image: "It is easy enough to say man is immortal simply because he will endure: that when the last dingdong of doom has clanged and faded from the last worthless rock hanging tideless in the last red and dying evening, that even then there will still be one more sound: that of his puny, inexhaustible voice, still talking. I refuse to accept this. . ." I blissed out, Faulknerized. What luck to live with Faulkner and Hemingway. But while I sat with my beer and *Times,* Papa was home in Cuba writing a sour letter to Ezra Pound calling Faulkner "a no good son of a bitch" and saying (as noted in Carlos Baker's *Ernest Hemingway: A Life Story*) that *A Fable* "was not even worthy of a place at Ichang, where they shipped the night soil from Chungking" (or not worth shit), and soon was writing other letters calling Faulkner "Corncob" and "Old Corndrinking Mellifluous," complaining of the tricks and rhetoric of the Nobel speech beside *The Old Man and the Sea* and adding that *A Fable* was (again quoting from Baker) "false and contrived: all a man needed, in order to do 5,000 words a day of that kind of stuff, was a quart of whiskey, the loft of a barn, and a total disregard of syntax." It was well-known even then, from a big *Life* magazine article, that Faulkner mixed whiskey and writing (Hemingway didn't, except writing boozy, ego-crazed letters), and I drank up this fact, hopeful that alcohol would give me access to Faulkner's auroras. I drove home ringing with dreams. A brief late afternoon thundershower passed over the Jersey meadows, leaving the countryside green and limpid. My blood bloomed as I saw a rainbow arching over New Egypt. In this bliss my Drunkspeare labored to be born. Born of a bitterness I never tied to alcohol but saw without veils that life deserved. Tricky with skids, murderous, tragic life. Beyond any rainbow, Drunkspeare was a death-silver image within me. He saw businesslike corpses walking about upright. He fed in a naked boneyard, gnawing away with an eye for the toothsome maggot, and grew strong on horror—a fearless seeker of the ugly and loathsome, to confirm his power to drink up the worst that life could offer. He was a painlover! a Spaniard for crucifixions, stickler for disaster, who looked for the brains on the fence when pilots went down in nearby pastures. His ambulance-chasing lighted up every nerve, put every value on the scale. Give him doom, oil-flames, fresh death, and his heart thumped. I felt twinned, joined forever to his grey glare. Something sang, a wordless feeling in the sunlight and sirens that the sunlight held unspoken just for me. A warning I could not drive off. A story took root as the day drained toward quitting time and first drink. At my desk my heart beat on. I saw the story clearly. My readers will be cutting their wrists on this one, I said, but I'll head for a note of Tolstoyan hope. This is my *Death of Ivan Ilyich*. Good God, can I really take on Tolstoy? My eye eagles my climax. Thoughtfully stretch and shake my feathers, and fold my hands on my desk, weighing an invasion of Russia. I'm gripped, no less than a masterpiece awaits me. Do I have the balls? And my Drunkspeare arises, answering over the five o'clock siren, You need a beer.

I dread telling over my four-year Air Force career—one

groan should do it. A drink I lifted in Albany, that public tombstone, in heartsucking hopelessness after being sworn in, was carried by night train to Texas and a barracks whose waterbugs thrived on boiling steam from showerheads, where a weekend pass meant heat, bars, beers, a pint of Old Crow from the state store, an air-conditioned movie balcony, blackout and splitting awake half-dead in midmorning watery air under a longbladed green ceiling fan in a strange hotel room shared with two airmen drinkers I couldn't recall meeting and never saw again, a drink I carried by bus in a bouncing foam of sex-hunger through the Southwest to my new base in the Mojave desert where my high irony was set aside for faceless newswriting on the *Jet Gazette,* and was carried again by Greyhound and with the same bus-rocked hardon from California to Carlisle Barracks, Pennsylvania and the Armed Forces Information School, and carried back again still by bus to Colorado Springs, Colorado, my two-thousand-mile hardon sensitized past bearing, my brain a green slime of booze-fruity sex pictures, the steady sips—blackberry brandy? muscatel?—the sips exciting hormones into steam on my brow, giving an insulin buzz to the testes, but at last I'd arrived at the Great Divide, its rise from the plains mightier than the inner grandeurs of alcohol, only to sip once too often and lose my light-drenched hour in blue Air Force heaven, having written a news piece from the base chaplain's anti-Communist Mayday broadside to the Colorado Springs Knights of Columbus, a pipsqueak blast lighted only by its quotes from Lenin, which I snapped together in a fit of pique, leaving out the chaplain's attack, and with Lenin in print next morning I found myself within the hour packing and transferred to the Air Defense Command station farthest from Colorado Springs that my public information light-colonel could place a finger on after bursting in spit all over my face, Presque Isle Air Force Base on the northernmost nipple of Maine, a teensy penal colony under thirty-foot snowdrifts, and once more bounding by Greyhound I carried my drink through a two-thousand-mile coma ripping with hormones, arriving at my base on the Canadian border only to be plucked free and transferred to Westhampton Air Force Base on Long Island, a resort village where drink ran heavy and I saw independent wealth at last, the goal made flesh, and a rough cow's tongue of envy ran up my back, I deserve, I deserve, then carried my drink into marriage and on my last transfer, to Maguire in New Jersey, where I wrote and edited the weekly tabloid *Fighter Scope* for a year and a half, fat, a father, with a handful of grey-uplift short stories written despite chemical overcast, taking chances with beer in my office afterhours, filled with a rage to live that covered a blood-rage at my powerlessness, no easing of desire, only more intense need to fill the pit beneath me with cock, obscenity, ego, food, sweets, and noble mindsharpening booze, and with a vow to work like a devil and seize my large destiny I downed my drink at discharge and walked into civilian life, ready for a refill.

Four years later, divorce over, thumbing about the country and holed up in a waterfront fleabag in San Diego, I ran into a friend I'd served with at Westhampton. Paul was a gaunt, sensitive young Catholic who memorized Dante in Italian (he was Irish), opened me to Mozart and liked a light wine on Saturday afternoon when we'd walk the dunes and chat. He'd just finished Hardy's endless epic poem *The Dynasts*, was amused by the poet's colossal guiding ironies, and now was reading the complete poems and novels, while I carried the twenty-two-volume Oxford World Classics set of Tolstoy everywhere I went while in the Air Force. He was in agony waiting to marry his childhood sweetheart and lived in a stupor of love. He had weekend duty one Easter and when I returned to base he told me of his ecstasy in the duty room on Easter morning. He'd been reading the *Paradiso* and the gospels. I was a Tolstoyan atheist who gave lip-service to Christian morality and believed in a Christ stripped of miracles. But Paul's glow moved me. He was the first believer in Christ as Son of God that I ever admired for his critical mind and book savvy. In tiny script he wrote sonnets idealizing his bride-to-be as Beatrice. This appealed to me. I forever idealized girls out of their skins. He probably influenced my first marriage. After meeting him I sometimes came back to the base drunk at midnight and broke into the base chapel for fifteen minutes of fruitless prayer. I got what I gave. I admired Paul's faith, and tried to imitate him with my wife when we did marry. Then we were parted by my transfer, and met checking out books at a San Diego library five years later. In our joy he invited me to dinner next night, he and his wife shared a trailer near a fairground. I'd bring the wine, being a missionary for my favorite brand. I arrived in my best clothes with a gallon of my California red, a fifth of the finest brandy I could afford, and a costly copy of the exquisite new von Karajan *Cosi fan Tutte* for his wife Marian. The dinner and drink swam by; they drank modestly, I did heavy work on the brandy and wine, left the heel of brandy for them and took the wine remains back to my fleabag. Boy, what a glorious night. I'd been in fine fettle, my road obscenities a bit uncurbed. No, less than a bit. But he could see how I'd deepened, sharpened, become a world mind about music and a creature of biting honesty, fearless of word before women. Bearing books and a winegallon in shopping bags, I stopped by their trailer that Saturday afternoon. Marian answered, not quite opening the door. "I have this for you," she said, and slid out my Mozart gift album still glistening in its royal satin box. "But this is for you!" I said. "Please don't come back," she said, "we really don't want to see you." "Won't you tell me why?" "Please just go." "Well, at least keep this album, I already have a copy." "No, I couldn't bear to play it." "Please!" "We don't want it. And we don't want to see you again. Ever. Goodbye." The door closed. The album wouldn't fit into the shopping bags and I walked back to the far bus stop overloaded, lumbering, glaring with shame. A boor, I'd been a boor! a roaring, brass-tongued boor! Even then, blistered and squirming, I did not know I was a drunk. All the American writers and poets I admired drank as I did. This shameful day

39

simply was a rare misjudgment, an asininity on my part I would not repeat. Somehow I'd take it in. But I choked on it, and when it came to mind I suffered. Fifteen years later, I forgave myself.

After my Air Force discharge we went home and lived at my mother's rooming house. My wife Norma got a job teaching and I was taken on as nurse-chauffeur for a well-to-do elderly retired plywood maker who had Parkinson's disease. I'd met my ideal subject in this shaking, stuttering, expressionless old capitalist whose body daily fought off the dimming effects of his nerve-drugs and calmatives. I fought and loved him throughout the fear-dreams of his last year and a half of life, stayed with him until he died, quietly drank up his booze and replenished it with money from his wallet, and wrote a short novel about him which became a chapter in *Sweet Adversity*, still under revision twenty-three years after I lovingly splashed it to paper. The splash no longer shows. This was the only time a winepiece of mine had a backbone worth recovery from Drunkspeare's mangling hand. But my crimes grew, I disappeared into far off Manhattan one drinking weekend, slapped my wife in a fit of high vanity, punched my fist through our bedroom wall, kept her from rest with overbearing midnight concerts, and drove her to tears until she cried *"I never know what you're thinking!"* and she filed suit. I never knew what I was thinking either. I lived on the forward surge of a Hawaiian blue comber of alcohol, that Dionysian grip on words I valued beyond wife, son, or even being published.

Single again, I lived with my mother, and broke down. No one saw it. Outwardly, I dressed like John O'Hara, and the homburg was back, a mask of self-esteem for my new job as daily reporter on our morning tabloid, the *Jamestown Sun*. We worked late afternoons and evenings, which cut into writing time but left comfortable drinking hours. I had some lucky scoops, feature stories not really news, which I blew up like Steinbeck, and had a shining sense of my skills. But I was actually a poor hand at covering lackluster Board of Education meetings and was forever outclassed by my rival education reporter on the granitelike *Jamestown Post-Journal,* a woman pro who took shorthand. I was often at half-mast for these evening board meetings, a half-pint of blackberry brandy or vodka in my jacket for wakeup sips in the wash room. Did I miss anything? I'd ask my pretty rival, who'd smile and coo No, then speed into her fifteenth page of hentracks. Christ, I look great in my old photographs from the *Sun,* mustached, debonair, a hardbitten gentlemanly glow and all teeth under my homburg. Meanwhile I was driving my mother's sodden old buddies home at midnight and trying to score, chasing widowed mothers of my old schoolmates, getting relief from housewives I'd interview in their homes, and using my job and costume for couch conquests and couplings on the livingroom rug with my clothes on for a quick split. Alcohol fanned sex and drew me into less happy, possibly criminal and certainly crazy acts I won't describe (my mother is still alive) but be assured that I awoke often under waves of shame and would rush out to rake the lawn, scrub the car and the hit the barber for a skilled mustache trim. In my long black overcoat and neat toe-rubbers I'd walk to work feeling the pale glow of leprosy, or stand with a half-smile at the library takeout counter and seem like an escaped forger. My pupils would not untighten. The winter trees knew my guilts. Even my friends' wives weren't safe with me. At thirty I fell in love with a fourteen-year-old and our affair flamed and flickered until she shot herself dead at twenty-six, the story of Cynara in my novel *Eternal Life* (which I wrote when finally sober). Drunkspeare was blooming, my stack of winewords filled a deep drawer in my bedroom desk, my winethumbed rejection slips were kept in a red velveteen candybox like heirlooms. I loved my death-notices (they were deserved, I *was* dead), would paper my walls with their certification of striving and failure, and had about five hundred before throwing the box into the East River one burgundy-wracked night. I felt metallic in Jamestown, running trembling and highstrung on diet pills, arsenical wine swelling my tongue every morning, passing out at the cafeteria table while taking lit courses at the local college. Escaping the typewriter I'd sit in a Jamestown moviehouse with my gallon and laugh the loudest laugh in the theater, a laugh horripilating to others as I burst with happy pain over subtleties no one else picked up on: I was that unleashed giggling snicker and booming hoohaw from the balcony.

My last New Year's Eve in Jamestown, Rob Grapevine and I chose to cap our celebration with pizza. Fifteen minutes to midnight and driving my mother's car, I hit fresh ice and thumped through a lamp post at the front door to the high school. We got out into wild sleet—and the big metal pole had vanished. It rested fore and aft the car roof. We couldn't move it and couldn't leave it. The blue bubble of a police car flashed and, wanting to save his family embarrassment, Rob said *Caramba!* and faded. According to my rival paper's account, "Newlove attempted to strike Officer Jerry Thompson after the accident." The night is sketchy. I think I said, "I don't want to go to the police station, I want a tow truck." The officers were mistaken about my driving, this was an accident. They thought I should phone from the station. I'd kept a tight rein, not wanting to look drunk, and slipped into my John O'Hara mask of hardbitten smarts. They said come peacefully, reached out for me, perhaps I slipped and grabbed Officer Thompson's arm, and next I was on my way in their backseat and then being stiffly walked into a big metal-walled cell after I'd wandered from the desk and been found in their lockerroom pissing down a shower drain. I let them know they had a gorilla on their hands. That metal wall rang with goon-song. I bellowed my ripest writerly obscenities down the hall toward the desk. Unmanageable rage. For an hour, I wasn't sane in that cell. When I came to on my steel wall-bed, my editor and my mother were staring at me through the bars. I was uncombed.

The Post-Journal writes up drunk drivers as a public duty, *Sun* education reporter drives through high school lamp post, and in fact they worked up four stories on my little skid, detailing the accident and arrest, my arraignment for drunk driving, lawyer's name, bail, trial date, failure to show up for trial, lost bail, license suspension and so on, one headline calling this the "Newlove Case"—that was enough. Another story headlined their lack of news (Trial On Drunk Driving Charge Not Yet Scheduled) and bolstered this with four fat graphs repeating all the old material, with a final note I felt was just for me and my *Sun* pals: "As long as six months sometimes elapses from time of arrest to time of trial but processing of cases now is much speedier than it once was, the court employe said." I forfeited bail, not so much to avoid a verdict of guilt (I had a black eye on leaving jail and pleaded innocent at my arraignment), but to save my life. I'd read the writing on the highway: If You Drink, Don't Drive. I'd passed out and run off the highway into a tomato patch with my three-year-old on the front seat. In a fit of sobs, I'd driven my mother's new car in blinding rain and lightning to the old Ripley graveyard one night to see my father's tombstone, which I'd never seen, and folded in her fender and smashed the taillight against a stele in the unlighted mud paths. And now I'd sent her new car through a lamp post, a third repair job in six months. The choice was heavy but also a deliverance: I'd abandon my driver's license, since I had no choice about abandoning drink. I did not drive a car again for fourteen years.

The *Sun* was sold to new owners. At a big party at a lakeside roadhouse, the drinks were on the washingmachine-millionaires who'd bought us, anything the bar served. I swore I'd stay sober and keep my O'Hara cement-fast. I got polished, a night not to remember. I was fired soon after. Thinking of the *Post-Journal*'s dance on my lost license, I asked Jim Fox my city editor—after I'd turned into a bright column of blood in the newsroom,—"Are they letting me go because of my drinking?" He looked surprised. "Oh no. It's that you can't double on brass. They need a feature-writer who's also good on hard news." Today I wish he'd lied and said yes. I knew I drank too much, and even at unwise times—more and more while working, and even driving I'd kept a fifth for strength. That fifth was hard to outwit, like keeping a crazy wife balanced and calm when she could go weird in a flash while I was behind the wheel. Much heavy breathing behind that wheel, and whenever I parked and switched off the ignition a billion nerve-ends unknotted in a flush of peace and safety. Sometimes getting home I sat in cold sweat feeling sparks relax in my crotch. I was at such times closer to God than in my midnight chapel reveries years earlier, experiencing a wealth of thanksgiving for having made it into the garage.

It was getting harder to breathe. A two-paper town and the *Post-Journal* wouldn't want me, even if I had the sobriety to master their fact-crammed style. Good God, that seemed living death! I was into a mad new novel that took every muscle of fantasy I could bring to it, a national mock-epic, *The True History of* PROMETHEUS *During His Visit to the States.* I borrowed some bucks from my mother, and went thumbing, both for research and to find a secret town for my now fifteen-year-old Cynara and me to hide in. From California I bussed down to Ensenada on the Baja peninsula, where I rented an all-stone room in a two-story concrete whorehouse called Hotel Pacifico #2, bought a bag of pot and gallons of cheap Mexican brandy and wine, and spent three paranoid weeks tight in my room moving my novel along on a rented typewriter. What a glare as I floated over those pages on sings of wong—oh, that pot! A whore in a candywrapper-purple bra stopped by for tokes in the brilliant cobalt mornings. I lived stark naked in my concrete room with the door open. Nobody cared. I was the only permanent resident, aside from the ladies treading about flatfootedly in aluminum lingerie. There was a stone shower to clear the brain fug and a maid passed through once a day to sweep the stone floor, which was ashtray and wastebasket. The toilet was a hole in the floor with two footrests. I sat in the near-bare room typing on the lone table, ego-swollen with mountainous chemical joy, rubbing my belly habitually, cock-stretching any moment I wasn't typing, finding I had a drinker's lisp while talking to myself (it stuck for eight years) and eying my eyes in the small sinkmirror, the cloud-shattered blue glaze that told me, This is worth everything.

Bussing over Golden Gate Bridge I wrote the last page of *Prometheus*, choking with joy at having ended a novel at last, its long song rising with drums and flourishes. I thumbed home to my mother's rooming house, dropping fifteen pounds on the face of the country I'd just ennobled, and cut the manuscript from 550 massively wandering pages to 333 of marching short chapters, typing all summer on Mother's back porch with my winegallon for coolers. My trim body soon bloated over my Bermudas, but the pile of chiseled, time-defying pages excused any manner of energizing that got the work done. "Energizing" was my fresh catchword for wine. I leaned hard on juice for playful spirit and mental breadth. Under the first noon sips of iced red, my fancy spread like clouds on the veldt, a babble of russet sentences I'd forcefeed with sense. Not a phrase failed its sunset glow or spurt of song. I sought a marvelous, sad, earnest Homeric pessimism whose gusto for tragicomedy rose above night and gave spirit by sheer energy. The novel took four years to write and is my best Drunkspearean work. I could still energize on booze and spring back from its daily slugfest. But the book is unfocused, willy-nilly, each page slippery lyricism, the rhapsodic plot racing over banana peels. After four or five rejections, I put it away for more mature revision later on and have not read it in twenty years. But it was earnest play, many single chapters had been enjoyed by friends, I finished it with a sense of steel and hope, and when it went unpublished I felt steeled to lack of success. I cracked and mended. But what next? After that epic I was a force hovering in midair without the underpinning of print. I must try for something shorter. The vision of writing another four-year novel, with the gusto and hope of *Prometheus* and of it too going at last into the trunk was too spirit-breaking to bear. I must set my sights lower for a brief masterpiece that would announce my glory. So I began a short novel, *"Les Quotables,"* a madcap sketch of the drinkers I'd read about in saloon society columns that had run in the *Sun*. Alcohol celebrities like Toots Shor and Earl "The Night Owl" Wilson attracted me, just as movie drinkers had when I was five, and I knew I'd done enough research on drink to see me through. And so my hero Prometheus shape-shifted into Dionysus, the great booze-spirit. At first saloon society seemed beneath me, but the fun took over, the manic vision powered by Dionysus himself. With that novel, alcohol drank me.

Each New Year's I'd tell myself, This is your year, Don. This year you publish. And the year would go by with no change, only more unpublishable stories and novels piling up, my Pan-spirit tempered in an alcohol forge. I grew strong on defeat. I was Hercules trying to lift invincible Antaeus whose mother Earth gripped his ankles. Only the myth shifted and I was the one whose ankles were gripped, my mind flooding with weird phrases that asked to be embodied in the sentence being built. Some bit of muddy brilliance I couldn't cast out. But with a deep breath I'd wallow on, longing to keep the clear mind I'd had just before my first drink. Before I'd drifted into the wine sparkles. I was bound by yearning, which I called "lack of nookie" and thought sprang from being unpublished, but what I truly longed for was a deep cure for chemical over-cast: to roll on the ground and cast off my ill spirit. I could not see the endless waver and strengthlessness of my life as I worked like a Titan to scrape the dead man's float of the moon from my spirit.

My beloved fifteen-year-old moved to Manhattan and Barnard and so I went too to be near my famous saloon folk and her. I shared a seven-dollar-a-week railroad flat in a Polish apartment building near Tompkins Square on the Lower East Side, hired out as an office temporary, and finished *"Les Quotables"*. About this novel I said literature be damned, this is a book *for me*, and will write itself. On wings of drink, it would be whatever I pleased and owe nothing to the well-made zombie works seeing print. I forgot this was to be my "breakthrough book." My nerves raged to see the most wholly self-satisfying *Alice in Nightowlland* I could write. My nerves raged, that lisp hung on like my bloat, and I was a shark about drink. It had to be hoarded and guarded; there was a me-first desperation about precious money spent on booze. An elephant howled within, its death-agony a call for comfort as I lived on memories of my great love, and on the joys of the bed she would grant me once every three or four months on a slumming trip down from Barnard to see what I was writing about her. I pondered castration, would it help? At last *"Les Quotables"* came to an end. I'd bloated out on ale and wine and supermarket specials such as three-pound packages of chicken hearts for 39¢ which I'd simmer in garlic and oil. That was the kind of money I earned, and yet this child of *Esquire* had an unswerving belief that he deserved the fancy watering holes of saloon society, "21," Sardi's and Toots Shor's—I was angry with myself for being unable to earn what I deserved, for having this cursed skill that couldn't turn a penny. It drove into me like a cakeknife, and if I wasn't dimming out on macaroni and cheese or spaghetti and chicken livers, the only relief was writing itself. Somehow, there was hope at the typewriter, a giant wide-carriage Underwood manual that demanded stamina as it spun out my life-threads. This spirit-machine was my girl and I licked and played and drew on her love with an arm like Casals bowing his cello, a hard bite into every singing phrase. I sat there, a smiling hysteric, through thousand-year civilizations of brontosaural waterbugs, racing roaches, silverfish and deathproof insects for whom the wonderpoisons were mother's milk. But I loved it, my street, my building, my writer's pad, my pastas, my spine turning to wine and even God seeming approachable each twilight, a nameless heavenliness forever teasing my fingertips. At a certain glow-level my brilliancies assured me I was an angel writing in Paradise. Perfection shone.

My mother sold her rooming house and moved to Florida.

A friend driving down told me he knew I could get a job in Hollywood, Florida, if I cared to go with him. Well, Prometheus needed a rest and could use some cash for a writing bankroll, so I went. I got hired as an ambulance driver. No knowledge of first aid, no driver's license required. The fall harvest of elderly moneymakers from the North turning into September corpses in Florida was upon us and the ambulance service needed every hand it could hire and worked us around the clock. Nervewracking, to drive at eighty, siren howling, no license. We carted the sick from home to hospital, picked up tooth-strewn bodies from car wrecks, plucked the dead in their infinite novelty from lawns, bathrooms, attics, wheeled them as if alive into emergency rooms (we did not diagnose!)—my hair rose when one motel corpse was my father's ringer. My deadliest job was wrenching a naked body from between a bathtub and toilet, where it had fallen upsidedown and stiffened, the blood draining into the bald man's purple head and chest, a wrestling match (talk about Antaeus!) whose cold horror lasted fifteen minutes, and as I got down and pried I told myself that if I lived through this, that then I had gone through my Guadalcanal, my Iwo Jima, my Saipan, my Tarawa, my King Lear tree-splitting storm, my Godot, my *No Exit*, my holocaust, my pie-slice of the universal horror and tragedy and that I was now an accredited Twentieth-Century Writer and fully empowered to seek and state the definitive negative statement for my times and to hold a mirror up to the power of blackness, the night within the night, my Dachau, Berlin, Hiroshima, a spiritual desolation that granted me the clear right to drink. I deserved to drink to keep my good cheer and avoid suicide. Good cheer, goddammit, at any price. I still, of course, didn't know I was a drunk or that my bottom was far, far off, and that I was now only groping about in my graveyard period, a merely literary agony. My own death-stiffness lay ahead.

Things got worse. I left the ambulance service and went back to my Lower East Side pad. My voice had got louder, so loud that I often appeared to be talking ahead of myself to cram in everything "important." My brain raced, buzzed, I couldn't keep up with it and tripped over my liquorish lisp and bit my cheek or tongue painfully at least five times a week. I'd get too hungry and at my first mouthful of cold spaghetti my teeth would sink into my lip, white stupidity filling the kitchen as I slammed down my fork and cursed. Whims, manias, compulsions, obsessions, thousands of movies to catch up on, skirts to chase into bars—I moved about like a ginspider and couldn't sit still long enough to write hello to myself. I carried two shopping bags wherever I went for ten years, for winegallon and books. I was bawling at the movies, the unattainable Leslie Caron in *Lili* shaking me with my all-time self-pity freakout, though dogs and horses too were always good for a few sobs. My long, wifeless years on leprous bedsheets were catching up, and even the sheets had burn holes like leopardskins. My sense of conflict flooded out in yes/no statements about everything: yes, things had never been worse but this was the best year of my life in many ways.

I gave up self-pity and crying at the movies, lip spiteful as Baudelaire's, and for two years buttoned up a big balloon of tears growing in my chest, unpricked but ready to burst and hungering to attach itself to any image. A woman's glimmering eye in a magazine would sock me with homefeelings for lost arms and ladies and leave me with my mouth open with thought in my rocker. Five, ten minutes would pass, even my glass not lifting. Biologically, I know so little about women; blue arteries in a Degas bather stir my deeps. Or a *Life* picture of a family wiped out by flood, a mother crazed by a War Department telegram, the conquering scientist who died for humanity—just show me some grief, I'm there, I'll suffer. I'm a Garbo addict, race about collecting Satchmo records for midnights on the red, I'm always stark naked in my rooms whoever visits, stubbing my goddam toe on chairlegs, but let me hit a funny patch in my work and I giggle, I snicker, my eyes run, I have a laugh that chills. Good God, am I in pain.

My spirit supports only short stories, each more bizarre than the last, with my still-denied pain showing through. Pain is the breath of art I call inspiration. In "The Naked Man" I fall to earth and try to live in society without clothes. In another I am "Bleeding Man" and go to Cynara's Riverside Drive Halloween party as an auto fatality with my head covered with ketchup (a true story). I buy a long box of teletype paper when my storylengths start doubling under drunken and longwinded bemusement with diamonddust detail. Up the street is a burned out building whose top floor looks intact and this appeals to me as a no-rent island paradise, so I set forth on a restrained realistic novel called *Eternal Rooms* (no tie with *Eternal Life*) about a black family in that top floor. *Rooms* goes nowhere when finished but into my eternal trunk. I dig out *"Les Quotables"* and decide to get it published by imitating John O'Hara, who got *Appointment in Samarra* underwritten by craftiness. I would take out a full page in *The Village Voice* and print the opening pages of my novel, with a plea to publishers. And so I did, rewriting these pages to a high polish, and under the effects of this brainstorm some of my visitors vanished: these were waves of unreal worms crawling under my skin when I lay abed, colonies of viral beings that looped and numbed their ways up and down my legs, little shufflers who weren't really there but heralded possible polyneuritis (a blanket term that covers many kinds of inflamed nerves). Now I was alive and glowing, zapped with hope, shaking. This was it, my year! I took the copy and hardsaved money over to the *Voice*, and soon they gave me a proof to correct. So that you may have a taste of the true Drunkspearean style, I give the heading. I'm afraid that the note with the double asterisk ** fails to refer back to anything.

PUBLISHERS, READ

This book is for sale to the best publisher who makes an

offer. It is the second of four completed books (Mr. Newlove's best is his first, "Prometheus," a damned good book, indeed, in sure beauty and big color.) Mr. Newlove can write.* Sure beauty in big color. Mr. Newlove is printing part of "Les Quotables" here to aquaint the reader with something new that is about to happen in his life and see everywhere (you bust the syntax.) Muscular publishers are invited to jump on the money.

Your Obedient Servant,
Donald Newlove

*Sure beauty in big color.
**He got beat up last night in a race riot and is not clear-minded as yet.

Nobody jumped on the money. No house answered, not the meanest paperback. Weeks passed. When I thought of my great page, my gut lighted and skin raced with shame. Ever naked, my burgundy heart ran like an icecube, I left bloody footprints all over the linoleum. Staggering disappointment could only be bested by a new novel. I'd write again for myself, and with even grander Drunkspearean ecstasy, and so I launched a novel about Garbo (Welles in blackglasses was the blind movie director hero of "Les Quotables") and of her affair in Venice with the beloved Frankenstein monster. What imagination! a dream subject . . . and I meant it to be the first high-class pornographic novel, something that had never been done—another original. This blue movie was called *The Rise and Fall of Boris Frankenstein*, or *Hardonicus Erectus*, and had only one shot at success: with Maurice Girodias at Olympia Press or else I was writing for the trunk. No novelist had touched the Frankenstein monster since Mary Shelley and I was eager to work my thumbs over his puttylike skull. I knew him intimately, or his heart, since he typed and swilled at my desk nightly until three in the morning. The novel also featured the story of Bob Bottle, his cock Boris and their attempts to bring sunrise to Bob's cold sexpot Cynara, my Barnard beauty. This wretched novel drank me all the way, its surreal syntax making "*Les Quotables*" look august.

Done, I hand-carried it to the Olympia Press offices near

Union Square. The sky was pink. I went home to my gallon, coursing with hope, and waited for weeks in my rocker, knowing that this novel was sure beauty in big color, very funny indeed, and sexy too. I was spending the money already, when a letter from Girodias arrived. He'd turned it down, the novel wasn't as strongly pornographic as he needed. I'd been too serious! With splitting groan *Boris* went into the trunk. What doom, to fail Olympia Press standards. The sky was grey. But after a few weeks my spring welled up and I impacted myself into a novel I'd defy Girodias to turn down. I could not bear failure at this level.

The new novel was *The Ice Palace of Doctor Faustus Brain* and tells of the chase of a mad scientist-art collector, who is as deformed as a Picasso figure, by a Life Force figure from Army Intelligence, Colonel Eric Kazantzakis. They find they are half-brothers, both illegitimate sons of Theodore Roosevelt. The Colonel has a Barnard paramour, Cynara, but the story's chief sex attraction is a three-hundred-foot giantess created by Doctor Brain from thyroid extracts and kept in an ice palace at the North Pole. I was set on being less serious in *Brain* than in *Boris*, and yet (drunken) filigree talks about art kept waltzing in, along with enriching nods toward the Tibetan mysteries of the Secret Doctrine and Madame Blavatsky.

And Girodias turned it down, and into the trunk it went without a try elsewhere. In *Brain* I was writing as well as I could and as the nights flowed by on gin and wine I knew the old ecstasy, and the pages were whitehot from the forge. But I was uneasy, noting gaps in sense I'd never meant and a new leaning on a kind of impasto phrase, "the breasts of frigity" and so on, and senselessly lovely paste-up sentences. A look back at a page or two from *Prometheus* and a pit would open: I'd dimmed. Was I a one-shot novelist? Would I ever have the ease and style to write that well again? I hadn't written one page as intense as *Prometheus* since finishing that novel. Fold failure in with endless sex-hunger and the self-pity throbbed, my heart a red velveteen box of death-notices.

Just before my Olympia Press moonshots, a friend mentioned hearing of a sick art-lover on Park Avenue who needed a nurse-valet. I got the job, working half-days for him and still writing. My boss was a Princeton student who'd left college after almost dying of polyneuritis, a result—he suggested—of his excesses. He'd spent six paralyzed months between life and death in an iron lung, and then one day found he could move his big toe. His father and uncles all died of heart failure in their early forties and, already in a wheelchair, he didn't expect to reach thirty. Obsessed by art and esthetics, he collected art books, etchings, and needed someone to wheel him through the museums, to his poetry course under Robert Lowell at The New School, and to help him dress, bathe and get fed. His first-hand insights into art in Europe and the States gave me a great lift and I agreed eagerly to be his private nurse on his farewell trip to Europe—if he could last until he got there. Off we flew to England, Spain, Italy and France. The scenery from this disaster fed into *Boris*, the paintings into *Brain*. He could sip only one drink or so a day. I did better. Our first night in London the news came that Hemingway had blown his brain out with both barrels of a double-barreled shotgun. That same weekend Céline died—his photograph hung over my desk back in Manhattan. So my summer became a boozy elegy, all Europe overcast, a long toast to Ernest, his gruesome death so hard to take in as I reread *A Farewell to Arms* and *Across the River and into the Trees* at free moments in Italy. The night after the news, I stood on a hill outside a London moviehouse, so blotto reading the poster for *Intolerance* that I let go of the wheelchair. Suddenly there was a scream, the chair racing for the curb at the corner. I just caught it. My funereal drinking came to a head in Barcelona where the low prices for booze stoned me with wonder. This was heaven, pennies for litres of anise and brandy. Within an hour of checking in I'd stocked a bottle of each in my bedroom. Bob, my boss, asked me to wheel him into my room so he could see it. "How much were *they*?" he asked about my bottles. "May I buy them from you?"

"Sure." He took them into his lap, had me wheel him to the bathroom, and then emptied both down the toilet. "Don, my life, such as it is, may depend on you. I've got to do what I can to protect myself from you. I'm sorry to have to tell you this. Try to keep me in mind, I beg you. I'm not much but I'm all I have!" Then I put up his set of black curtains for his afternoon nap and went back to my room, shaking, mad, ashamed, and witless at just having seen two full bottles of booze poured down a toilet. This ached, like an act of cruelty toward a child.

Back in Manhattan I was so mocus and swacked with sentiment at seeing my friends' faces once more, that I stole a dozen jars of caviar, boxes of top cigars, and big artbooks to wrap as gifts for my fellow underdogs in the arts. The store and front window seared with light as I came out of the Eighth Street Bookshop, a Skira artbook under my trenchcoat, dropped it into a shoppingbag, then hit Marboro's across the street for a second glossy art-giant and hustled gleaming with joy back to my Seventh Street pad. Wine had spun me into uttermost sentimentality. Gifts in pretty wrappings piled the kitchen table. Why hadn't I ever thought of giving friends presents before my spirit-deepening trip to Europe? I sit with a fresh gallon of red in my rocker and glow at the kitchen. Christ, a dozen tins of Japanese smoked oysters and I'll be set for the season. What success! I light up an Antonio & Cleopatra, put on my European soundtracks for *Jules et Jim* and *8½*, and rock my great soul with Jeanne Moreau and Fellini. Within a week I'm nabbed boosting a kid's game leaving Brentano's, questioned by a store detective in his office and told not to be seen in the store again for five years. He had me cold but read my face and saw Drunk.

Supermarkets should support American literature, I thought, especially its living writers. Either I was too good at stealing or theft was so heavy that it was cheaper to let the food go than hire teams of lawyers. Rob Grapevine stopped for a weekend on his way to Mexico. The silver-overcast Saturday morning he arrived we were into a carefree gallon when I decided on celebratory steaks for lunch. A&P would provide, I told myself, and asked him to enjoy a glass and some Bruckner while I shopped. I was oiled. It's not sane trying to get out the A&P door with ten dollars of meat stuffed into my chest until I looked like a circus fat woman. I'd been grinding my teeth all night, every night, hearing knocks at my door with no one there, and my mother in Florida speaking my name from the back room. *Donald.* What? I was sick (no one knew it) and perhaps trying to get help through strange acts. Once more I was being interviewed for shoplifting. This time the cops were called. As the store manager took me out to the street to wait, I broke loose and dashed down an alley, escaping. But not really, since I lived only a block away and avoided that corner for years until a new manager came in and only one old lady clerk remained from the day of my fiasco. I owed money everywhere anyway and could go home only by a chess game of shady streetcrossings.

Without notice I dropped out of all my jobs and disappeared into myself for my first long binge. My clothes scraggled and beard went to spikes. My nerves hopped, I shook, my eyes were wired to a far thought I couldn't think. My prose dropped its Olympian standards and bitched up sentences were given a shine and allowed to stand while I worked through first drafts that became unrevisable last drafts. When I read these works to captive friends, sitting at my desk, jolly, fat, plainskinned Don Newlove, their heads fell, rolled with weakness, boredom, fluttering stares. A missionary for Shirley Temple records, I played mine without pause. An ordinary day became a holiday, wining with her, despite off-color echoes and the desires she aroused. Beneath my left rib cage my liver flipped and shivered like a dying fish. I'd watch it shake my fat, try to settle it with a half glass of brackish red, breathe deep, breathe deep, breathe deep.

So I drank wine in darkness.

A call from Cynara got me passingly sane and back into temporary typing so I could take her to *Tristan* and Burton's *Hamlet,* but when these sparkling weeks died I bought a rifle, holed up with a case of gallons and meant to kill myself, my slow-time apartment a weedy seabottom. I was beyond writing but hanging drugged and naked over my typewriter was a change less boring than the choking self-pity and swamplike hallucinations on my bedsheets. I'd jumble type down the page, pick away at some scalelike glitter, slip into maggots and sores and pus, black-spirited but ravished by small flares and flowings and phosphorescent rottings. Not I, it was the alcohol writing, seeing, feeling, fingering its own small squeezings and surges, poetizing all by itself, my colorless brain ready for any drop of dye. I'd wake up on the floor, unable to tell by the window whether it was five in the afternoon or the morning, timeless as a zombie. Never had I lost heart to this depth.

But rent, rent! my Polish landlady pounding my door. So I followed a lead from a fellow drunk and got a job reviewing books for the slick book-chat weekly *Idle Hours,* edited by Bob Bookfeller (the staff called him Bishop Bob). I was being paid four dollars a book and thought myself blessed. What could be easier! The books often came as sets of very long, bulky, unproofed galleys, bitches to handle. As I got better at it, my pay went up to five, then six dollars a book. But income was never equal to habit. On my weekly payday, having written five reviews and collected thirty dollars, I'd shine my rotting shoes, press my crotchstinking, shinyassed pants, trim the fray from shirt and jacket, knot up my best greasy tie, pour down a tall wine or two for ballast, then subway uptown to The Forum of the Twelve Caesars or The Four Seasons for one costly drink amid the greatest elegance available to me, *burn* for one brief moment! I hoped for a triumph of decor over loneliness, never knowing one person at these palaces. Drift over to Toots Shor's or Sardi's and nurse a cheap beer while eyeballing for celebrities—was I waiting to be discovered? Then my bright hour of class-drinking would be over for the week and I'd hit an

Eighth Avenue fight bar for its special half-price watered giant double martini and go home to my gallon, refreshed and ready for music and writing—suffering but happy that half my pay was left. Money still tight, I'd double up on jobs, go typing down on Wall Street or at some billing desk in the garment district, and take home half of what the typing service was paid for my work. I made $1.25 an hour, the minimum wage, but that was better pay than book-reviewing. Saturdays I'd rise fresh and early, wipe the rooms down fore and aft, stock the icebox with six or twelve big green sweating quarts of Brewer's Gold Ballantine ale, balance my Underwood with its gallon of red, and by ten-thirty be shipshape for A Whole Day's Writing. Keep the juice at bay, don't get smashed, this is Bare-hearted Writing. But by one-thirty I can barely keep my chin crooked into my thumb as I await from heaven the next Mallarméan bloom, the Saturday afternoon tree of alcohol branching and flowering over me as in some secret place in the country, blue cigarette smoke creeping over my private trout pool. I am home.

And with a jerk fall sidewise, dreaming on a puffed up marshmallow adjective, until another jerk wakes me about three, drooling, and my chair squeals wretchedly as I stagger for an icy refrigerator ale, and rinse down my withered tongue as the brew belches fresh stabs and throbs through my brain fissure and I hang in there for a few eternities of utter hangover. Glaring at my Underwood, I find two or three sentences have come together and need only one daub of mist to become poetry and I soon rejoice over three bars of neon made from my inmost gauds. The ale lift dies and I'm fastfalling into still another snooze, awaking to a Brewer's Gold like warm piss. This story's not moving, that's the paragraph I started with at eleven. I better rest, maybe review a book. And now the wine Titan is really tested. Writing drunk is hard but reviewing drunk is like staggering under a corpse chained to your back. Pick up a long glassy galley burning with lamplight no matter how I twist it—and moan! it's some dreadful Revolutionary

War or British naval novel or (I'm quoting myself) a tale about "the golden nightmare and efflorescent decadence of the Roman Empire during Caesar's heyday" or a new comic novel "that has the continuity of a marijuana jag and the esthetics of a belly dancer." Starting first pages of these galleys is like trying to run up the face of a cliff. Flog myself to force one sentence flowing through my brain. SHOUT OUT THE OPENING SEN-TENCE. But it would self-erase. A fresh mug of red may help, but let's keep the pot in the desk drawer or I won't get through page one. The wine robs me of speed, so I leap whole chapters, fake the middle, and try to rebuild the novel from its last chapter, if I can grasp even that. Drink makes me cagey. I'm superperfect on detail, evince a rolling sense of the novel, give it my hardbitten honest judgment, and meanwhile purify the page, clean copy at all costs, erasing into the wee hours, fearful of being shown up as—*sin of sins!*—not having read the book. But my long-fought burgundy aurora borealis would slip into sentence after sentence as I admired "the greatest review I have ever written." And I'd expose myself blindly, a few wines fueling me, gallon in bag, sublimity level glowing, as I met my deadline and handed in a smoking bolt of criticasting. Bishop Bob would read it, look up in wonder, and say, "Donaldo, I can't understand a word of it. Do you really mean what you're saying here?" I'd blush to the roots, hold my breath to keep the air fresh, and race full tilt to the defense of my follies. Try to imagine defending this reject—it was never published:

The Candy Butcher's Farewell, by Leslie Goran (his name was Lester but I didn't get even that right), Sept. '64, McGraw-Hill, $5.50.

†††A novel from heaven, written by six angels using one hand and remembering the wallpaper of every house they grew up in. The style here is an improbable, poetic meld of Isaiah and the arch cuteness, in the best possible sense, of Capote holding his youth in his hand like a baby mouse. The story carries Henry Sneffer, Jr. through his boyhood up to his eighteenth year in 1945. Henry's mother was a "nurse," that is she lived with men

mainly for money. When she died, Henry was always searching for his father. He goes to live with his Uncle Jonas and Aunt Alma, who are sublimely accumulating their tenants' pennies. Henry's high school days as a basketball center are related with a zest that will make Salinger slap his wife's wrist with pique. Henry's eyes are wild windows of imagination. Eventually, he finds his father, who is a candy butcher (sells Crackerjacks and "dirty" pictures) at the Mystic Theater in Atlantic City. His father absconds with $1700 for the Miss America contest, "the candy butcher's farewell." This beautiful, beautiful book has built-in perpetuity, by a writer whose love of life races like a street full of marriage horns and streamers, whose eyes know the details of all our remembrances, and who writes with broken glass in his fingers.

Our style allowed a Maltese cross at the top for an impressive artistic work, say *Dr. Faustus* or *A Moveable Feast.* Three Maltese crosses could herald only "a novel from heaven, written by six angels." I'd clearly had a sip and a toke, Goran's page pulsing with rainbow slush as my backbone got disneyfied with glorious marimba music. Trust a drunk to be excessive. I was in spinal bliss trying to forge through the first chapter and never read the book, then tried to bridge my reading gap with blinding praise. At the office I had to stand for ten minutes inventing defenses for my gross overwriting. Ah, that this had happened only once! Or that I'd learned from it. But once monthly I'd have to unknot some review strangling in its praises, stand before X-ray Bob, my ruby-colored mind striving to pluck sense from senselessness, a world-sigh spreading underfoot as I defended my idiocies against his merciless nitpicking. I was aghasted by his insights into books I'd never read, and admired his keenness. He had book smarts!

At home I'd sit dying in the red throb of my sunset heart, as the addict Francis Thompson put it, and sniff flavorous perfume from the strawberry shaped soap I kept on my desk for a quick lift. What could Bishop Bob know about the fat old bacchante I became at times on my bed, the god of chemical poetry a blue flare licking my skin? And I'd float off on a little lecture to him, You should watch my liver if you want hair-raising objectivity. And I'd prop up the damned galley to read it "again," finding out what it was really about, and slowly shame bubbled and leached me grey as I faced writing a straight review that would not show me up as a cheat in my first notice. I'd now be hard-pressed to get any of my heaven-storming into the nutshell that befit the book. Often, my new shot was taken and paid for—and a second reviewer's notice got run. Mine was untrustworthy, despite two tries. This bracing setback would find me writing spotless, time-eating reviews for three of four weeks until I had good footing and—gasping in a wine bind—faced the need for a fast curve. So fast he won't see it! I'd steamroll some cliché-monger with thirty books to his name, flatten him so thin he'd wonder when the war began. If the book wasn't worth reading, neither was the review and Bishop Bob could safely skip over it. But how to level a just damnation on this wealthy, job-free world-traveler without reading his numskullery? My failing was restraint: I wrote to kill. Without warning, reviewing the money not the book, my javelin pinned the bastard to his bank vault door. Even falsely, I killed better than I praised, got a laugh, and saw my kill in print. And shaky letters handwritten in white anger or splotched with typos would arrive at the office from Bermuda or Spain, suffering hacks wondering why life had fallen short of their hopes. Bishop Bob stood by me, writing back that into each life a little rain must fall, even in Bermuda and Spain. Usually I was overly scrupulous—stoned by conscience—when reviewing through a mist; would purposely sleep for a few hours on the floor to get sober, then yawn through the dawn straining to meet my deadline. It was very, very rare that I got a floater by Bishop Bob, and he had a flawless eye for a fast one. His patience with me was as endless as his own run-on sentences. I, of course, was an active alcoholic, could not learn, nor stop my bizarre eruptions.

But my chest was splitting as I bit back spiritual jaundice, or now adored my tangerine glow, echolalia and tintinnabulations, the authentic rhetoric of the true drunk, its shadows and ironies, universal overcast, the last red dingdong of doom breaking ecstatically over a dying landscape. I was a Dachau camp scavenger waiting for a windfall package from a book club, a heartbreaking lifesaver to cover a gallon. I sent in every book club coupon in print and for the most expensive books. Clubs adjust for losses and never sue. Nor would I open their bills. No books might mean a trip to the blood bank or, barring that, and with my store tab hitting the stars, actual drought. I had a Spartan heart for those drinkless evenings and knew I could feel better for the abstinence. Just thinking about abstinence could make me feel better. Suddenly I could unshackle my chain to the next drink. This proved I was not an alcoholic. I did *not* have to drink every day, I'd decide, and on my way in the rain or a below-zero blizzard become buoyant about even a rockbottom typing job. I was not going to drink today! I might even start singing in the flurries, radiate my good will over newfallen snow, and sit with idiot smile on a wet train to Wall Street.

A gray ocean lapped at my window. And then a woman fleeing her husband came to live with me, bringing her three-year-old daughter and baby boy. From the pit I rose overnight to become semi-married with a nursing mother and little girl. I'd not lived with a woman for ten years. The change into standup breadwinner had me beside myself with luck, sending up silent prayers of thanksgiving, feeling tough and strong, giving my reviews serious thought, and launching into a novel worthy of my talent. The rooms bloomed like an erotic hothouse all summer, a sunburst of poetry got read aloud, there were dinners with streamers, wine, and late, late candlelight. The new novel was my best since *Prometheus*. And then her husband found her. And she was gone, running off no one knew where, not even her parents. (Years later we met in Central Park and I found she'd gone to earth in Seattle, a city she'd picked blindly out of my atlas.) I fell apart. But to

61

keep the pieces in one place I wrote a full-length novel in three weeks about our life together, *Rainbird and the Gypsy*—an apocalypse of self-pity. I said I was writing for myself (a sure signal of self-indulgence and hysteria)—it went directly into my trunk, being too runny to mail anywhere.

When asked about it while writing *Rainbird* I'd grin with just bearable pain and say I was "doing my *Romeo and Juliet*," a phrase of Hemingway's while writing *A Farewell to Arms*. My masterpiece trunked, I crumbled. I found myself hanging around men's baths and swimming pools, but I'd wined out, hopelessly gross and unattractive, with stunned eyes, a small tight mouth and strawberry boils. Failing at the baths was even worse than failing at Olympia Press. Then Larry Bucetti, a "leading man" in underground movies, took me to Andy Warhol's factory near the Grand Central YMCA to be in a movie (I play "Lana Turner's film director" in *More Milk, Yvette,* also known as *Mr. Stompanato,* a film of fixed boredom and feebleness without equal), and I wrote up the one-day production schedule of this epic at enormous length. This became my first published work, filling nearly the whole August 1966 issue of Paul Krassner's outrageous magazine *The Realist.* He paid me $75, after I found him, and I carried the check into the street like Joseph Smith bearing the gold tablets of Mormon. I was *in.* IN! More meaningfully today, this was the work in which I surprised myself by openly stating I was a drunk. It just came naturally as I typed the lead:

PROTHALAMION FOR WET HARMONICA AND JOHNNY STOMPANATO

by Donald Newlove

I arose from a drunkard's bed and went into the city to witness the birth of Andy Warhol's first musical venture, *Mr. Stompanato,* a tuney love saga based upon the unfortunate death by violence of Lana Turner's paramour—in drag *and* in reverse drag.

By reverse drag I mean that Lana's daughter Cheryl, who

did the dirty work, is played by a small, graying boy (silver hairs by Clairol), while Lana is played by the undisputed Queen of Underground Movies, Mario Montez. The reverse is also that Cheryl is played as a boy, Lana's son-daughter, named Cheryl. They're in love and damn that nasty Johnny for trying to seduce Cheryl.

At thirty-six and still unpublished, I'd be asked, What do you do? Oh, I write. What have you published? Well, nothing. This was like being a thirty-six-year-old actor who has never been in a play: one smiled up from the well-bottom of self-esteem, squinted for dim stars in daylight. That smile took tireless electricity to overwhelm any hint of being a horse's ass. Meeting fellow writers I'd burn with casual superhuman intensity to mask my poor memory for names ("that woman I married"), powerlessness to follow even the simplest talk (I'd focus on some squib from Mars to add to our chat), and haze over a publishing schedule that resembled pale winter afternoons in a leprosarium. All that was at ten in the morning, sober.

But my visit to Warhol's factory spurred visions of myself as an underground movie director and through a severely overblown statement of income I pried a thousand-dollar "moviemaking loan" from Chemical Trust, got a Chilean crew together and began filming my as yet unfinished *Trumpet*, an uplifting but rambling quasi-documentary about trumpets in Manhattan. From weeks of shooting emerged a still prettily imaginative three-minute Von Stroheim technicolor hymn in praise of Cynàra, my sometimes paramour (who'd married twice by now but starred for me), some twenty reels of as yet unedited trumpet footage, and a woeful account of our filmmaking which appeared in *Evergreen Review*.

With this fiasco under my belt, I returned to the great novel that was meant to restore me to the luster of *Prometheus*. I'd had a six-month stint as a social worker in Spanish Harlem's wretched Metropolitan Hospital and hoped to use it as background for a metaphysical medical flight, *The Body Artist*, a hammerblow work bursting in cloud upon cloud of black humor and bronze gongs of language. This novel took six powerfilled months to draft, and went through revisions past count. I locked my grip to the mill wheel, and milled, and milled. My heart was set. *The Body Artist* was my *Hamlet*, my immortality taking a shape, a demoniacal tragi-comedy worth every unexperienced brilliant summer afternoon dropped into its midnight, even worth stretches of abstinence from alcohol as I labored over Hermetic mysteries and symbols, pored through occult dictionaries and swam with the Secret Doctrine—at any cost keep the crucible at full boil. My hero, Brando da Vinci, a research surgeon who had never lost a patient, would outleap *The Magic Mountain* and *Doctor Faustus*—both!—in two hundred pages. This was my drunkest hour. Even not drinking I was on a chemical boost and trying to shape clouds born of wine, and I could not let go of them when into my sober years, with *The Body Artist's* failure clear past self-deception. I still had faith in the Drunkspearean sound, its bird song and purling ravishment, bliss of self-love. Drunkspeare would not die easy.

Houghton Mifflin thought if difficult, too eccentric for them, but that it would find its way. Hm, a last revision. I awaited good cheer to lift me. It wouldn't come. One more revision! Six months! Still, revision helps wall out the world, keeps the focus on work at hand, not dreams. And then, choking, Six months! What about the rent! *and the back rent!* The years dwindle down, Don, you're middleaging rapidimento. How about real life, that place out the window? Or hornblowing? You have no gift but a year's study, a little Dixie group . . . do I really want to spend my sunset years blowing "When the Saints . . ."? Brando da Vinci and Prometheus shrunk to a bandstand? Say another ten years flee by, only a few flurries in the magazines to show for it. Might be some nice cakes and ale *out there*, marriage, house, family. My good cheer came up on wings of pigshit. That I'd drunk myself into this corner I couldn't see. I just sat rocking under a chemical manhole cover. Then I took off to visit my mother in Florida.

We got drunk. I fell into a frenzy and beat her. I tore out her phone, busted her lamps and waded into her again—her suckling baby, her schoolboy, her brilliant son the class vice-president, her military school cadet, her Marine, her college student, her married son, her airman, her son the father, and then her divorced son, her unpublished son, her drinking son the reporter and carwrecker, her whoring son back from Europe, her fat bearded son in Manhattan, and her mother-beating son, heavy legs in bermudas, puffy eyes without pity—trying to slap her into sobriety and salvation. Who was I beating?

For the fifth drunken time in my life, I was thrown into jail. In the morning the jailer came and led me, clubbed and stunned, hair flying, next to naked and barefoot as a shithouse rat, from my cell. We went into an elevator. Utterly silent, it seemed to fall on foam. "What's happening?" I asked. "Your bail's been paid, sonny." I knew he was pulling my Yankee leg. The doors parted open like cobweb. That marvel of a bailer stood before me, not a foot away. She had a black eye.

I was now almost two-hundred-and-fifty pounds, red-faced, losing my hair, given to cankers and bleeding gums, pissing so often I'd use the kitchen sink instead of the toilet, finding my teeth and nails loosening, a victim of boils, my eyes were pink, tired, dry and scratchy and the lids stuck together with mucal infection when I slept, my ears rang and were supersensitive to any scrape or screech, I gave off a staleness no soap could reach, my crotch and privates were forever raw and cracked, I was losing the hair off my shins and pubis, my bellybutton stank and I shaved my armpits to no avail, my nose enlarged and capillaries split, the insides of my ears were raw from flaking, my tastebuds wore smooth at the rear and grew apart up front so that I oversalted everything and could awaken before breakfast only with a tablespoon of salty redhot pepper sauce, my skin eroded in the creases and rubbed off in balls, I had a relentless belch for years from an ulcer, a liver that was trying to get out of me and die somewhere, shitty shorts and wine gas that ate holes in them, breath that even I couldn't stand, sweaty cold soles and shoes I hid under the bed or in a closet if I had a girl overnight, I gasped during any kind of work and could not get a full breath even while typing, I began waking up nightly on the floor having convulsed out of my bed, wine trots were common and many hours spent near tears trying to wring out my bowels on the toilet, my pulse seemed to clog and dribble, I had false angina in my upper left chest regularly, someone was going to shoot me in my rocker so I moved it away from the window, but I had a waking dream for ten years of my brain exploding on impact, I would lie unable to wake up but not asleep while strange men moved about my kitchen and livingroom (they weren't there), I could not sit comfortably in any position, I smelled of stale semen between my weekly or biweekly baths, my gut bubbled day and night and I'd try to overfeed it to sleep, I had a two-year sinus cold and special flu attacks that laid me out near death, I was hoarse and kept grenadine and lime syrups and pastilles for my hack, my memory self-destructed on the phone and I'd hang up wondering whom I'd talked with or what arrangements we'd made, I often cried out "I'm coming!" when no one had knocked and I answered or heard the phone ring when it was long gone for nonpayment, I felt fungoid and sexually impotent for two years, I slept poorly and kept a pot by my bed in case I couldn't make the sink, I heard people laughing while I was trying to read and metallic sounds that echoed, my overswollen brain rolled liquidly in my skull, I got dizzy rising from chairs or picking up a handful of spilled coins, must I mention mere headaches and hangovers, my bloody morning shaves with safety razors, the mental fog that had me leaning on the table trying to remember my middle name, my age or where I just laid down my glasses, my rage over a dropped spoon or lost paper lying before me on my desk or the endless drinking glasses snapping to pieces in the sink, my poor handling of kitchen knives, and the strange yellow bruises that wandered up and down my arms and biceps, my harsh nerves and weird fugue states on paralyzingly gruesome images of loved people, the living dead people standing around my bed for hours on end (they're worth two mentions), and just normal things everybody had like wanting to sob all the time, especially over the sunset beaches and bathers in the vodka ads, divorced wife and kid, any lost piece of cake or life or unearned joy as a pretext for just letting go with a thirty-minute screamer on the couch, and such clinical loneliness that my cat talked to me. When this happened one morning I thought I'd had a break-through on the language of animals and couldn't wait to test my powers on a dog. Loneliness? I sprayed my icebox firetruck red and pasted it solid with a collage of breasts. When I filled it tight with big green sweating quarts I'd embrace it in a sex act. I had eleven cats and kittens and they all died in a two-week plague. I tried to hammer the last suffering big one to death on the roof ledge but its head was solid bone and so I threw it still alive six flights down into an empty lot where it turned with a broken back until dead. Music corkscrewed from my bedroom wall. Until my middle thirties I'd detested fantasy and lying to myself, then one night I gave in and was lost, allowing myself any sweet dream under my roving finger palps. During better times I took two hundred acid trips, stocked hash, grass, speed, peyote, psilocybn, and kept a moon of opium like ground figs in my icebox. Barren of drugs, I'd grind up morning-glory seeds from the hardware store, down them hulls and all with wine—they were hallucinogenic in those days (no longer)— then sit for hours in nightwinds under a hard bright moon and watch blue clouds unshadow Tompkins Square Park, loony as a June poet. And much, much more, I was a universe of unrecognized symptoms, fighting down wine, throwing up

67

through my nose, fighting down more and thinking I was happy. Why go on? Let's get to my real life—although I don't deny I had some time in heaven as a drunk, even after the booze got to me, which was fairly early, fifteen or so, or maybe I should date it from my under-the-bridge blackout with my hometown Marine buddy in Asheville. It doesn't matter. I denied it all the way.

A friend I love and think the finest poet on earth visited me sober one day. I hadn't seen him for a year. He said no to a drink or pot. My God, I'd been following his footsteps for years as he wrote his way down into a thick deathwinged melancholy whose deranged glory grew ever drunker and more brain-damaged—I wanted to be just as despairing and ironic and was ready to die for it right behind him. He could make a four-liner cough with despair.

> *After you're gone*
> *The dusty miller will eat*
> *The carpet flowers*
> *In my furnished room.*

When he was leaving I asked him, Christ, why do you look so good? He'd joined a fellowship of recovering drinkers, he said. But gave me no pitch. That looked useless. As he told me later, I was the most hopeless drunk he'd ever seen, aside from himself.

A girl almost half my age agreed to marry me. A year or more later, as with my first wife, I fell in love with her. After six months of married drinking (she drank from a thimble, if that much, even when I tried to wheedle it down her), I'd vowed to reform my gallon-a-day wine habit and switch to moderation on vodka. This would help me lose weight too. We lived in a sixth-floor walkup and with my memory-frazzle I was forever racing downstairs for a toothpick and stopping to breathe three or four times as I carried it back up. Then came my twentieth failed transfiguration into a social deinker, as I strove to keep off wine and stick to gentlemanly, less fattening hard stuff. My wife and I both got paid on the same Friday and had a bundle to finance my resurrection. As we stood in the doorway of O. Henry's saloon, wherein my wine devils were to be cast out and higher proofs made welcome, and I stared at the pretty bottles behind the bar, all the drinks I could not afford since stealing them from my mother's liqueur cabinet a lightning-flash ago when I was fifteen, suddenly a cloudburst of self-pity hailed down on me, I cried aloud, stabbed, could not catch my breath, staggered from the bar doorway and fell in tears over a car roof, where I sobbed for ten minutes as if my pet gorilla had died or lost his black cowboy hat. I find shows of passion on the street embarrassing. Next day I tried recovery.

During my first meeting at the fellowship of recovering alcoholics, I burst into tears three times as the chains dropped off.

These were hardcore recovering drunks mostly my age. I sat and listened and got lifted and became a vitamin missionary and slipped back into pot and drank and sat and listened and began speaking at meetings and got drunk and sat and listened and became a shining knight of recovery and drank and sat chastened and listened and wrote articles about getting un-pickled and drank and sat and listened and smoked pot and drank and sat and listened and hit bottom on another visit to Florida and sat and listened and at last got active in my fellowship and got sober after five years. I'd been failing because of my hole card. I'd be getting out someday, when my ship came in. Paramount or Book-of-the-Month Club would give me a ticket to Spain and Drunkspeare would spend his sunsets on mild whites and rosés. I had not really joined the fellowship. Five years and I was still a tourist, a sneakthief of dry days, a time-serving thumbtwiddler, unwilling to face my evasions, not yet bleached to the bone, not yet ready to reach out to some nameless drunk at the other end of a phone call, not ready, not ready. To my backbone, not ready.

Not ready to join body and soul.

Getting unpickled meant recovering my life from the fog and looking at it. I didn't believe I'd been so bad, possibly I wasn't even a drunk. Or clinical alcoholic. Just a heavy drinker pulling back before deep illness gripped me. Plenty of hope, look how easy it's been. Just focus on good food, vitamins, cut down on salt, sweets, caffeine. What's so hard about feeling good, with sleep and a fulfilling sex life . . . The lifegiving lift of taking alcohol out of my body, that alone was the main work to be done, as was shown by my superhuman energies, tireless head for reviewing, vigor for order and sharp edge to my eye and sensations. Harps rippled, health bubbled in, I went into superlight—a shining blindness of pink clouds and romantic overload. I felt "powerful, fearless, surprising," as Kafka says of the writer when his spirit is moving. A man who sheds a chemical manhole cover he's been humping for twenty years can't help wanting to bound over light bills, the rent and bourgeois piffle. True life is real magic—spinach and iron!— and Giant Despair lies with his skull cracked in the sunwash.

Me sober, I want write. Three months of recovery, reviewing, and remarriage pass but not one page appears for the stalled revision of my Hamletic *The Body Artist*. When set aside, Brando da Vinci was locked into a psychic impasse and bitterly fat body, my pages black masses of jammed invention. Now, while I raged with health, Drunkspeare writhed and was held fast by a black glove. So I romanced myself and toyed with the thought and delicious smell of a stick of dynamite pot to break out of this dry spell. A fierce image of a pot seed bursting with Guatemalan sunlight gripped me, the visionary power, lift and magisterial overview one toke would grant. After three months sobriety I deserved a boost. One breath and I could invent the sun, puff new life up da Vinci's nose. Get him moving! my hand powerful with hard inventiveness. Christ, I needed a lift. Look at it rationally. Once through the novel, no more pot. I didn't care about pot anyway, hell no, my problem was alcohol. I could handle pot. Truth to tell, I wasn't really a drunk either. That's just something I faked to please others and for a romantic image and to get rested and recharged. I'm in a bind! Me no write. I couldn't see the simple truth: I wanted to drink more than not drink and would invent any excuse, or swear by any forgery, to raise my fumy and magnificent twin from his black hole. I could smell him breathing life into my Underwood, giving a burgundy intravenous to da Vinci. This is heavensent—the need for a fearless, powerful, surprising end for a work that will strike like a thunderclap when published. Good God, hadn't I even got dry at times to write certain passages? Could I be more serious than about this work? It escaped me that I'd been trying to finish with a dry mind a work born dripping with misery. A mere three months and I was supercharged, no longer a benighted man in a pit. But I thought I had to write from the pit as a Twentieth-Century Writer. And that *The Body Artist* was the just, pure expression of a kind of holy blackness I admired as the richest resource for dark language ("All flesh is grass"), a fearless gaze into the unhuman, the way Shakespeare relishes fingering Yorick's skull and hitting off lines an inch thick with grue. I was split-minded, forever psyching myself up with an endless health pitch while longing to conjure with darkness. What appealed was to be one-minded, coasting on red and working like a mason at my "breakthrough" book. Meanwhile I was in mourning for Drunkspeare and didn't know it. The crepe was blinding, weird urges to sob hit me from behind—my novel would *die* if I shilly-shallied much longer. It takes heart to march through a novel! What confusion. The one solid fact was that a joint would help me finish. Then I'd have my greatest book done, or at least a workable next-to-last draft, and be free to—well, why not accompany these few joints with a writing gallon for this big crashout to the death scene. Be hung for a sheep as well as a lamb. I stopped drinking too abruptly, I should have tapered off while ending this book. And in my heart of hearts I knew I was not really a drunk. I'd got sober for a lie. I was unique and had unique problems. What's more, my fellow recoverers bored me, the meetings bored me, they were not intellectually gripping. Nobody talked about art and music and writing, the stuff of craft that wholly engrossed me without relief. Even my small talk about movies was about craft. Like Edison working round the clock to invent the light bulb, the talking machine, the moving picture, I spent every moment I could wring from my waking life to think about art—and longed for more time, for a move perhaps to a stone hut in Iceland, or to the utter loneliness of a houseboat, with candles and kerosene. There was a dream, satisfaction unlimited, an orgy of solitude. I'd get sick yearning for it, my own place beyond the petty disasters of burst shoelaces, lost keys, bitching bills. Some Shangri-La beyond missed subways, where all space would pivot on my writing-time and I would suck on a happiness grander than booze. I longed for little else, aside from my drugs (gone, alas). At times I'd hear my wife chattering away down the table or across the living room or beside me on the bed. She'd become more interesting, a creature who shared my life and apartment, but I detested her unbearable self-analysis. I was above self-analysis, thought it a curse. She was a twin and shared with her sister a total brain transfer daily by telephone, the entire content of her mind scooped out and shrunk to electronic impulses. And she had two best friends with whom this was repeated daily, and an analyst she saw five times a week, and then there were twice-weekly comments about her from my analyst. I amazed myself by deferring thought about art to joining in on her self-analysis. She was *minced:* two analysts, a novelist and dream-reader (me), a twin, two intimate friends, and her own high intelligence, all focused on her (she was only twenty-two) as she emerged from the formless waverings of adolescence. This placed a formidable rival in my writer's household. How many Hamlets can one apartment support? Well, a few joints and a gallon and mad clacking on my Underwood should get the focus back where it belongs. I was far, far from recovering my life from the fog and looking at it, or taking inventory of my shortcomings, mis-deeds, and injuries to others. Still Big Baby, fighting my thumb.

All right, Brando da Vinci's stuck in a wordjam, should I blast him out? To help me slip, and slip hard, I reread Norman Mailer's bravura drug-piece on how he finished *The Deer Park*, or as the piece is called in *Advertisements for Myself*, "Fourth Advertisement for myself: The Last Draft of *The Deer Park*". A self-described "psychic outlaw," Mailer chose to live at the hard existential edge of egoism and honor, taking his kicks for extreme public statements and kicking back. After the second draft of *The Deer Park* he was tired, badly tired, his liver sick and depleted (it had gone bad in the Philippines during the war) and exacting "a hard price for forcing the effort against the tide of long depression," and Rinehart had broken its contract to publish the novel although it was already in page proofs. Mailer sent the manuscript to ten more houses, himself the amateur agent for it, "Machiavelli of the luncheon table, fool of the five o'clock drinks. . ." and he was making a few of his harder decisions on marijuana. In Mexico, depressed and with a bad liver, he'd been given "a sense of something new" by pot and he smoked it on and off in New York. The sharkfilled publishing world released in him a murderous need for survival, and he "mined down deep into the murderous message of marijuana, the smoke of the assassins. . ." He says ". . . marijuana opens the senses and weakens the mind. In the end you will pay for what you get. If you get something big, the cost will equal it." *I'll pay, I'll pay!* I thought, lusting for a mercurial glow to *The Body Artist*. After three years work, and a year away from his page proofs, Mailer looked at his novel and found its porcelain style and Irish adventurer-narrator not well-joined. Revision of the galleys led to a new typed copy, itself soon heavily edited. (Boy, did I revere this "advertisement.") But the first flood of energies passed and he found himself revising in a fever, fatigued, hungover as if with a "junkie cold" waiting for him, "loading and overloading what little centers of the mind are forced to make the hard decisions." Soon, he says, "I was forced to drive myself, and so more and more I worked by tricks, taking marijuana the night before and then drugging myself into sleep with an overload of seconal. In the morning I would be lithe with new perception, could read new words into the words I had already . . . the most scrupulous part of my brain too sluggish to interfere. My powers of logic became weaker each day . . . What I wanted and what I needed was the quick flesh of associations." But

> . . . the attrition of the drugs and possibility of failure began to depress me, and Benzedrine entered the balance, and I was on my way to wearing badly . . . With each week of work, bombed and sapped and charged and stoned with lush, with pot, with benny, saggy, Miltown, coffee, and two packs a day. I was working live, and overalert, and tiring into what felt like death, afraid all the way because I had achieved the worst of vicious circles in myself, I had gotten too tired, I was more tired than I had ever been in combat . . . there was only the worn-out part of me to keep protesting into the pillows of one drug and the pinch of the other that I ought to have the guts to stop. . . But I had passed the point where I could stop. My anxiety had become too great. I did not know anything any more, I did not have the clear sense of the way things work which is what you need for the natural proportions of a long novel. . . Like an old man, I would come up out of a seconal stupor with four or five times the normal dose in my veins, and drop into a chair and sit for hours. . . I would work for an hour, not well but not badly either. . . Then my mind would wear out, and new work was done for the day. I would sit around, watch more television and try to rest my dulled mind, but by evening a riot of bad nerves was on me again, and at two in the morning I'd be having the manly debate of whether to try to sleep with two double capsules, or settle again for my need of three. (From *Advertisements for Myself*, G. P. Putnam, copyright 1957 by Norman Mailer.)

Later, the manuscript at the printers, he took mescaline and unexpectedly wrote the last six lines of the book. "And it was the only good writing I ever did directly from a drug," he says, "even if I paid for it with a hangover beyond measure."

Well, if I needed a sanction from an older, bold, respected writer, this was it. I missed the whole warning at the end, of course, a peculiar blindness wiping that out for me. A few sleepless nights had never hurt me yet, his agonies were glamorous, and marijuana still had the kick of a royal flush, was not easily put by without a sense of loss. My recovery could wait a few weeks while I hobbled into destiny on my grass crutches. I dug out some "forgotten" Dominican weed from behind the icecube trays. Hopped to my grog shop where I'd not been seen for months and raced back up the six flights. I must get this going before my wife comes home for dinner. Light up, pop that bottle. Strip naked and let the evening begin!

Sniffing, her arms full of groceries, my wife sneered from the kitchen doorway. There stood Old Purple beside my desk, shoulder glistening, hemp-smoke layering the rooms. Her sneer swerved into tears. She sat down breathless on the couch, her wrists and fingers knotting over her knees. Her teeth ground silently. A hope that had been building for three months, through diet books, vitamin cooking, keeping herself attractive and accompanying me to my fellowship meetings, much pumping up of my handsomeness at the breakfast table and brown-bagging my health lunches for me, sober evenings spent in candlelight and the taste of the salt of salvation in our lives, burst. To me she shone, her arms and miniskirted legs writhed with loveliness, her face intense as never before, her birdbright blue eyes and cheeks and mouth vivid with love-hate. I sensed her very bones under flexing muscles. I felt really alive and committed as I rose with pale criminal bloodlessness and spoke my needs, for the brief loftiness of pot and boost of red to see my novel through to its rebirth in heaven. I saw stifled grief, small heavings of pain, deaf ears. Be reasonable, I begged, my guilt writ large in her anger.

Well, buster, Drunkspeare said, you showed her who's lord of the manor.

And he turned to his work until supper was ready. The meal was quiet. When it was over she said I would have to start paying more of the expenses. The blood shot to my head. I started shouting through a red haze. No, she said, if I planned to go back to drinking, I'd have to share more fairly on the bills, be more responsible. She would not support my habit for me. I explained, with towering restraint and patience, that this was a short-term drinking episode, for the love of a novel that was dying, and was no extravagance in our *detestable* budget as it now stood. I really did not enjoy discussion about household economy while trying to float my heavenborn novel to port, so *I* would not think about any change for the moment. I needed a last forced wine march, merely at maintenance level (pot did not bear comment), and would be through in two weeks. She said her suicidal low self-esteem was not helped by helping me drink. I put my side with louder humility. I'm sorry you feel that way, she said, slicing off my bag. I could not shout down her sincere good will or suck her into argument by rage. Her eye said I was sick.

"If I had the money, there'd be no argument, right? This is a money fight!"

"We'll talk about it when you're not drinking."

"We'll talk now, Jackie. I can't sit and write with this goddamn sword hanging over me."

"What sword?"

Speechless. "Do I have to spell it out? Everything you've said!"

"What was that?"

"You think I'm Einstein and can remember all of your feminine relativity?"

"Then what I say isn't important, so why talk about it?"

"Of course it's important."

"Can you remember the last thing I said?"

"You said—what did you say?"

"I think I'll go to a meeting."

"*You* go to a meeting? I'm the drunk."

"I thought I'd try the meeting for mates of alcoholics."

"Why?"

"I might enjoy it."

"Somebody has put you up to this."

"I need help."

"It's that fucking doctor of yours . . . Well . . . 's gone on too long already." I stared at my typewriter and felt my writing time fading into still another night of analysis of her problems—but pot always released some monstrous honesty in me and I loved tissuing our finest feelings.

"I'm going."

The door closed. I looked at the time-wasting dishes, the typewriter, then closed my eyes, breaking down. I stiffened in sorrow, loving her, jumped to the door and ran naked into the hall.

"Thank you!" I called down the stairs.

She looked up. "What for?"

"For going to the meeting. I love you," I added, smiling through bruises we'd traded.

"Don, I'm going for myself, not for you."

". . . I'll leave the dishes in the sink."

"Do as you wish."

Lights out in the kitchen. My Drunkspeare, arise! But as I stared at the page, even Drunkspeare saw a novel vastly awry and misshapen, beyond even his bubbling ingenuities. Still, I had infinite faith in his powers of revision—he had a genius for placing error—and could not bear the agony of setting aside my greatest work because my ending was feeble and unworthy of my Faustian (or Promethean or Hamletic) hero. Well, Goethe spent thirty years ending his *Faust*. I wasn't out to copy him, only to drape my polymath with spiritual black velvet. These artistic problems swept me with an inescapable insight: it wasn't fun anymore. Finishing *The Body Artist* was work, not play, an act of will, not imagination. The fellowship of recovering drinkers had plucked the very heart out of Drunkspeare. He was now more of a golem or zombie than a force of bursting spirits. The fellowship had fatally ruined my wine rider, now that I drank against knowledge. Not much knowledge! but enough to know there might be a more fulfilling way to write than sitting drunk at my typewriter. Perhaps I did not need a brain full of maggots to invent the sun.

My body sat rolling joints, sipping red, staring through pot-glare at shifty lines of types, scratching its damp crack which could never get dry even with baby powder, blowing on thin, delicate glories of artifice while pulling out boogers and trying to sit so an itchy pile wouldn't itch—yes, it had all come back! the brackish taste as the wine line rose up my gullet, the bathroom lurch, the winethumbed page and spill on my desk papers, greasy elbow on my chair arm, pot-gagging and lush eyeballs, gas, the open-mouthed slowing down that for me meant Writer at Work, waiting for the bass warble. The window darkened. The street clatter faded, sirens far off. I was home—but not home. A kind of television camera in the corner was recording the clinical life of my body. No matter what gesture, leg scratch, or cavity I sucked, the film played it back at the same time, showing me apart from myself. For ten years, living alone and ignoring my worst habits (aside from my brief uplift and new life with my runaway gypsy and her kids), I lacked any head for seeing myself as another might see me in my three-room den, and was even a bit proud of certain slovenly habits that showed my imaginative side at work, my brow knotted like Brando's with forethought and art, gut uttering bullfrog belches, lungs fuming deep drafts of tobacco smoke, my piss call a naked wall to wall passage to the hallway toilet. Now, like Robinson Crusoe after all those years alone, I found wet footprints that weren't mine leading from kitchen bathtub to bedroom. And I saw my own bare body, the naked man at the desk, myself the barbarian, and a last jutting belief in my powers and need for writing at any cost wavered, crumbling at the edges. Was it possible I really was hopeless? Wouldn't success and money allow me to walk upright, recognized, and to write with ease without booze? What success, what money! This was the same chair I'd itched on for ten years! A sandbank gave way in my chest. I saw the drained, ghastly drunk returned once more, unable even to sit upright or type one phrase without erasures, his body the pale belly of a beached fish, death-freckled, a whine of self-pity coiling him and choking all hope as he gripped his Underwood and wailed side to side with pricked pride. I went berserk. The kitchen window stood open to breezes. I lifted the enormous widecarriage machine, staggered with it into the kitchen and dropped it six flights out the window. It landed on concrete in the garbageway between buildings. Then I dropped Old Purple, still two-thirds full. Suffering violently, I eyed two huge cartons in my back room, stuffed with twenty years of rejection slips, notes, love letters, stolen diaries, photographs, and bills without end meant for embodiment in the Great American Novel, got dressed, carried the boxes downstairs, went back up for our shopping cart, wheeled the boxes to the East River and dumped boxes and cart over the steel railing into the river where the half-sunk armada went floating toward Liberty Island in the moonlight. As they hit the water a tremendous string had burst in my chest, almost cracking my breastbone.

I stayed dry for eighteen months, going to many fellowship meetings. Some of the satyr gleam shrank from my face and I shed five years of flab from my spirit. I became a saint of high energy, vitamin-pusher, fount of health chat. Touch my hem and the spirit would race up your fingers. I needed plenty of front with my fellow recoverers since I still stored pot in my icecube tray, to my wife's disgust. It's so hard to keep a gloss of honesty with your wife while hopping up the roof for a joint or dropping acid or mescaline without mentioning it to her. Just like a closet drunk, I'd struggle not to lisp (pot did it too) or talk stupidly and would be pleasant and active, the soul of companionship, do the dishes, and then drop off into music. Music was my invisible cave, hers was the telephone. She smoked nothing. I'd strive to overcome pot glaze with a Tolstoyan steel stare that insisted I was straight. If I smoked in the apartment, where I most often smoked my pot, we often fell into a whole evening of analysis, which left us raw-nerved, and then into bed where the pot had its famous effect of delaying climax. I thought the erotic power of pot so overwhelming that I could not give it up, that without alcohol *and* pot life would be prison-striped. I enjoyed the camaraderie against alcohol in the fellowship, the jokes and inspired humor about drinking, but at bottom I raged to drink. And I romanced alcohol, kept thoughts of it active and perking with talk about the tastes of various drinks and my lust for a cool draft on a hot day. I was an encyclopedist of booze flavors, soft drugs and pot varieties. I knew I would leave the fellowship someday, when I could afford to become a gentleman drinker, and until then I'd drift by on smoke. The idea of leaving the fellowship was not openly admitted to myself; I simply knew that I could not go the rest of my life without alcohol as my staple of daily euphoria. That just could not be. I had never been able to avoid hypocrisy about my vices, but about ardent spirits I was as certain as the turning of the earth. I would drink at some unclear future appointment with my Drunkspearean shadow.

A story taken by *Esquire* never appeared (it was returned two years later), then I lucked into a Christmas dinner at Robert Lowell's home, wrote that up and *Esquire* printed it. One day an editor called me in and asked if I'd like to do a piece on Tennessee Williams, who was reportedly in and out of clinics, with horrific health problems. He was now at The Plaza, why not interview him and do a headpiece. Truth was, the magazine had a sheaf of Fellinilike color pictures of Williams and his home in Key West and needed some copy to justify running them. But my ego began swelling, I agreed, and went home to read the complete works of Williams as well as memoirs about him by friends. Despite the profound booze-daze and befuddlement of nearly everything I'd written so far, I'd become an alert student of alchemy and reader of Jung, and my journey through Williams made me hyperaware of symbols—Williams leaves himself open to this by borrowing Greek touchstones. I was undergoing a sea-change at forty-one, and eager to grapple with phosphors and strange seabottom glimmerings in the unconscious, as if my slow release from the fogs of booze had granted me a new sense for the depths of words. Through all this my real fear was not of falling flat with the new piece but of reentering the world of alcohol. For nearly two years, I'd been avoiding active drinkers and did not trust myself loose in the bar world.

Williams was to receive a gold medal from the American Academy of Arts and Letters and I went uptown to the ceremonies to meet him. He sat on the stage between Leopold Stokowski and Allen Ginsberg, wearing black glasses. When he wove off his shades and gazed about himself, he was half-lidded with dry red eyes, looked dusty-tongued and buzzed with barbies. Lillian Hellman spoke a defense of Tennessee in his long fall from grace with the critics, saying he'd be remembered in a hundred years though turned against now, and a standing ovation greeted his Gold Medal for Drama for 1969 award. Tennessee rose from his camp chair, and pressing his groin like a fouled boxer, hunched sideways in a slow-bombed dream to the lectern. Draped like a crippled pitchman over the lectern, he said, "*Heh, heh* . . . Uh, I think I'm essentially a humorist, y'know? As I'm going to try and tell y'somethin't'make y'laugh—I hope it does—and if it doesn't then Ah'm no good!" The audience took this like a breeze over warm corn-pone. "Perhaps most of y'know or at least've heard of Maureen Stapleton. Well, one time she received a phone call from a friend of hers who said that so-and-so was gettin' married and M'reen said, uh, Who's she marryin'? And the caller said, Why she's marryin' that, uh, *that man*, you know, he's a homosexual." He looked just splintered enough to tell a dirty story. "And M'reen, uh-huh, and M'reen said, What about the bride? And, uh, the caller said, Well, of course, we know she's a lesbian . . . And then the caller said, You know, they're not even bein' married by a real minister, they're bein' married by a minister who's been de*frocked* . . . And Miriam, uh, Maureen, said, Will you do me one favor? Will you please invite

Tennessee Williams to it'. . . . And the caller said, I didn't know Mr. Williams, why should I invite him, Mir—*Maureen*? And M'reen said, Well, he'd say, 'They're just plain folks!'" Without adieu, Tennessee turned and hunched on shredded-wheat biscuits back to his seat. He'd barely acknowledged and thanked no one for his medal, not even Lillian Hellman for her introduction.

I stood on the terrace by the Bacardi tables, surrounded by the fabled gents I'd long aspired to join, when Tennessee strolled toward the drinks like a con man who'd sold one blue sky too many and felt the sheriff on his heels.

"Mr. Williams!" I cried down to him at boy-level.

He looked up, smiling suavely through Delta sunsets. "*Yezz?*" he lisped.

I dropped a net of mutual acquaintances around him. He listened with spongy goodwill as I finally asked for an interview but slipped like jelly through my net. "I'm not very good at interviews any more," he said. "I'll send your magazine a story or a play sometime." And he headed for the punchbowl, swirling back into himself.

I wasn't a bit discouraged. I'd prepared like Hercules for this interview and, by God, if I couldn't get through to him, I'd invent my own Williams. One of his friends had warned me, "Don't let it throw you, that first impression—he's always where he's at. Key West or Manhattan, doesn't matter, he's in his own little circle of light. It's the pills." Little pills Williams called "the phone numbers of God."

What unsettled me wasn't Williams's resistance (he couldn't bear to be touched physically and his agent found it difficult to get in touch with him even by phone) but the possibility that I might have been wrong in my estimate of his work. At that time I thought Williams was writing the best works of his career, that his *Kingdom of Earth* was a master-piece, his *Slapstick Tragedy* tragicomic genius, and that *In the Bar of a Tokyo Hotel*, far from being self-parody and a fiasco, was his great Crucifixion play and an inspired, religious work.

And if I had not believed those things, I would never have written the story, since it would then have been only an autopsy. I saw him in a process of transformation only great artists must pass through to achieve their summits. And these summits are universally neglected or misunderstood for decades after the artist's death. I cited to myself works Schumann wrote between hazes of madness, and Eugene O'Neill's nerve-shattered physical decay and mental state when he wrote his greatest play, *Long Day's Journey into Night*. At that time O'Neill was washed up. What first attracted Baudelaire to translating all of Poe was that—for the first time in his life—Baudelaire heard a fellow sufferer's hallucinations as his own, while Poe was dialing the phone numbers of God in Baltimore (on his drugs of choice, of course).

My own pot smoke was building up and I had a warning dream, in paranoia tremors and glimmers, of the rat's feet of alcohol scuttling through my unconscious. This dream was brought on by a story that Bud Lee, the photographer whose pictures I was illustrating with copy, told me: "When I was first down there in Key West about a year ago and went to Tennessee's house for the first time, Tennessee poured me a whole glass of gin with only some drops of flavoring on top and said, 'Drink this.' And I said I didn't drink. And, wow, that was the wrong thing to say, because then Tennessee says in this ghostly satirical voice, '*He* doesn't like to drink, my, my, *my!*' Boy, I felt like a horse's ass. So this year when I went down, he offers me a whole glass again and I drink it all right down and immediately get up and pour myself more. Then I made a horse's ass of myself a different way. Those people are so touchy and insecurity-ridden! You have to watch every word. They don't like anyone who's too goody-goody and doesn't drink."

Tennessee was at the end of what he later called in his *Memoirs* (1975) his "Stoned Decade." Nothing in print can equal the real horrors, not for me, not for him.

When I phoned Bill Glavin (Tennessee's secretary-companion) at The Plaza and asked if he'd shown Tennessee a

83

long letter I'd written him praising his new play and giving a close reading of the text, Bill said that he felt that Tennessee "wasn't ready for it yet" and had been sick in his room with a cold for two days, not leaving the hotel. I knew about that cold, once having had one for two years.

That weekend *Life* magazine came out with a gory full page ad in the *Times* that was a statement of Tennessee Williams's professional death, *Life's* way of advertising the fearlessness of its play-reviewer. Reviewers universally found *In the Bar of a Tokyo Hotel* subbasement Williams with very few flashes of genius. *Time* was kindest: "Still, there is an axiom of the racetrack that a thoroughbred will eventually revert to form. One must never forget that, despite his present aesthetic humiliation, Tennessee Williams is a thoroughbred." I thought everyone had missed the play's symbolic content and healing glow. Its barbiturate glow was only too bright and hallucinatory.

Coming out of the premiere of *Midnight Cowboy*, I found myself sitting opposite James Leo Herlihy, who enjoys a father-son tie with Williams in Key West. He was with Paul Krassner, my old editor from *The Realist*, and we were on an empty bus. Herlihy asked if I liked Williams's work.

"I find his latest plays since 1960 his greatest, those most panned and least successful. The critics want showshop and he's through whoring and wants to be true to his virtue."

Herlihy said, "Oh, that's swell. That'll do him good to hear. He's been very depressed about his recent work."

"Hey, what about his conversion!" Krassner gloated— Tennessee's conversion to Catholicism was reported earlier this year. Krassner was in high glee.

"Ha ha ha!"—Herlihy. "*He was stoned!*"

"He was high when he did it?" Krassner asked.

"He wanted a little miracle, I guess. Then he didn't get it. He doesn't go to church anymore. I think he's forgotten all about it."

Later, at The Church of St. Mary's Star of the Sea in Key

West, I interviewed the Reverend Father Joseph LeRoy, S.J., who baptized Williams into Catholicism (he'd been Episcopalian), and he told me, "Tennessee had been at death's door, and felt that God was calling him to become a Catholic." He added that Tennessee accepted everything in his profession of faith, "even immortality." Williams had then been fifty-eight and smashed thrice that year by flu, really at death's door. Even as I was writing up my piece on him, he'd left New York and was in Miami's Mercy Hospital, again flattened by Hong Kong flu.

Meanwhile, a New York daily reported on a strange message, penned on the stationery of Manhattan's L'Escargot restaurant, which was mailed to Tennessee's younger brother Dakin and started a one-day manhunt for the missing playwright. Disappeared from his Manhattan apartment! The message: "If anything of a violent nature happens to me, ending my life abruptly, it will not be a case of suicide, as it would be made to appear. I am not happy, it is true, in a net of con men, but I am hard at work, which is my love, you know." Dakin worried until Williams phoned that he was safe. Bill Glavin said the disappearance was all "a ghastly mistake." Tennessee's mother, Edwina Williams, in her middle eighties, chuckled in St. Louis. "My son has done such things before!" Well, yes, we all send letters we may not have thought through fully and that cause dismay.

While I was there, a lady puppeteer in Key West told me of going to a party at Tennessee's small frame house: "There sat Tennessee with a man on each arm of his chair. He smiled at us like a Buddha, as if he had a needle in his brain which just turned up the smile and left it there."

I phoned Herlihy, who said, "I went up to The Plaza today and he's been four days in bed with the flu. *I* couldn't even see him. He's hard to see even when he's well. It's that Asiatic flu."

"Does he ever discuss the religious content of his plays with you?"

"Sure. He reads them to us and we talk about them."

"I mean the esoteric content."

"Well, I think *that* is unconsciously delivered to him . . . that it's passionate and natural rather than intellectual."

I phoned Tennessee in his Plaza twilight, his long week indoors broken only by dinner with his agent. I gushed about his new play but he had not read my long letter to him about it (though he thought he must have). I said I knew he'd been ill. "Well-l," he said in a bed buzz I'd awakened him from, "let's say unwell." A distinction I planned to remember. Again I tried for an interview, but he was leaving for Missouri. So I reread *The Night of the Iguana* and studied its Christian symbolism. Williams himself was born in a rectory, greatly admired his minister grandfather, and was raised in a Christian atmosphere, so that this symbolism comes to him almost effortlessly and is, in fact, home territory. I felt pity for Tennessee, spaced out in The Plaza drapery with his play dying. All that money from the backers, sinking—because he wanted to write a poem to God.

A last shot, I phoned Bill Glavin at The Plaza. He was very warm—"I hear you had a talk with Tom last night." (Tom is Tennessee.)

"Yes, very pleasant."

"I don't know what to say. He hasn't been feeling good and today he's going to read in the *Times* that *In the Bar of a Tokyo Hotel* is closing."

"I thought it wouldn't close until June 21st."

"It says 'Last 6 Performances.' "

"They often say that."

"But tell that to Tennessee when he reads it at lunch today. He won't want to see anybody."

"I'm very high on his work."

"I know you are. I'll take your letter to lunch today and make sure that he sees it."

Phoned later. "Gee, Don, Tennessee finally read the papers at supper and he's not well."

"Bill, I understand you're going to Columbia, Missouri, where Tenn will receive an honorary doctorate. Perhaps that will pick him up some."

"Oh God, Don, you've no idea—Columbia will be *something* to live through."

I saw Tennessee's Plaza twilight transported to Columbia.

Why am I going to Key West? I asked myself 35,000 feet above the Atlantic and headed for Florida's tutti-frutti paradise, or colossal Men's Room for cruising by the U.S. Navy. I slipped into my purple Drunkspearean sunglasses and the Caribbean cloudlands froze into violet marble. I was stoned. In the Miami airport I'd gone into a liquor shop and bought a pint of one-hundred proof Old Crow rye, then in the men's room found I'd lost all taste for rye—it was like sipping metal polish. During the week before the flight I'd made a point of not mentioning my trip to friends in the fellowship—I didn't want anyone talking me out of my choices, to drink or not to drink, smoke or not smoke. So I knew at LaGuardia there'd not be much fight. I was shipwrecked before I boarded. In this final hop from Miami to Key West in a small prop-driven plane, I'd wanted to experience the little flight just the way Williams had so many times for thirty years, perhaps from this very seat. I stared at Dionysian cloudscapes through grape lenses, vast lunacies of gas split by brass shafts, a child's harmless coloring book, the heartbreak of the gods. Purple pulp.

Evening, I went into Captain Tony's dim, shrimp-net-hung saloon to check on Tré (no last name), an intimate of Bill Glavin's. Pet monkeys chattered. A beautiful blonde in almost no dress waited on sailors. My guts slumped, I'd no heart for this interview. I ordered a creme de menthe from her (Tré), poured it down, and had a refill. She was svelte, even if nearly nude, and told me, "What Tennessee really does is work. And drink. Sometimes Bill stays with Tennessee and sometimes he rents his own pad, depending on how bitchy Tenn is being. Bill gets him up, dresses him, does his secretarial work and when Tenn is smashed for the evening, Bill puts him to bed, usually about ten or eleven. Then he goes out for his own evening or to his own pad. But Tenn does work, religiously, every morning. I think it was Don Madden who told me that when he was playing in *The Milk Train Doesn't Stop Here Anymore,* in the

London production, when Tennessee did his revisions in the morning they were excellent. But after the noon martinis the revisions deteriorated until there were two scripts, and finally Tenn told the company, 'Just throw away whatever I give you in the afternoon.' "

The rye was undrinkable and in my pursuit of authenticity I bought a fifth of Wild Turkey (101°), a pint of Bacardi white rum and a pint of Southern Comfort and back in my room washed down a psilocybin pill with some wild Dominican smoke. Turkey, once my favorite, tasted like death—or formaldehyde, long-unfamiliar Southern Comfort was liquid cess to my tongue, and raw Bacardi a mouthful of brass pennies. The hallucinogen began to lift and the pot billow. At last I twisted and mellowed and scraped into *something* like the way Tennessee felt day and night—when he wasn't in the hospital—and my higher centers dimmed out as my brain turned to sculpted Kleenex. I sat awhile in my bare room, a Christmas tree lighting up string by bulb-string. Then, clubbed by the many hints and asides about leper colonies in Williams's plays, I spent the night leper-crawling from the Cave In to the Jungle Club and Cecil's Bar and Sloppy Joe's Bar (pictures of Hemingway everywhere, the local celebrity) and wound up at the Windswept Bar, asking along the way for directions to the leper colony. Nobody knew. I met many gargoyles on the Camino Real that night, made propositions to waitresses and was propositioned myself by a whitehaired old loon in ultraviolet white shorts and T-shirt.

"Well, I'm looking for a whore, frankly."

"I'll do anything."

"You can't do this. Anyway, I'm not at the mercy of my prostate."

"Well, you *should* be."

"Yes, well I'm not. I'm a fairy."

"I'm a fairy!"

"But an entirely different fairy: My wife has the purest fairy spirit you ever saw, and under the Napoleonic Code what she owns *I* own. D'you know where the leper colony is?"

"The only leper colony in the South is in New Orleans."

"Don't bet on that!"

Bombed puppet, I went back to my little white ship in the night and stared at the ceiling fan, rum by my bed, hope over ice cubes. I fell asleep and dreamed I stood under a tree taking a drink. My first bottle in a blue moon. As the booze ran over my tongue, a cloud of jubilee-sized maggots dropped out of the tree and stuck all over me. Awesome but not painful. I couldn't squeeze a single slimy maggot between thumb and forefinger to pull it off. I saw another man standing beside me under the tree and he was covered with maggots, but they didn't bother him. He was a leper and squinnied at me sideways. Tennessee, just standing there rotting. That's all right for you, I said, but I'm through dying.

This wakened me and I emptied all my liquor into the sink.

Next morning I felt like phoning Father LeRoy to attend my deathbed conversion and give last rites. Paralyzed. I lay between two worlds for hours, awake, dead, and groaning. I had never ever suffered such massive hangover. Hunger finally drove me from my spikes into the street. The sky was white as aspirin. A piss-elegant faggot passed by with toy poodle on a leash. I envied the little nipper his clear brain. Then I phoned and got invited out to Tennessee's house by Danny Stirrup, his house-sitter.

Danny and friends at Tennessee's had been drinking round-the-clock Thursday through Sunday when I appeared. Danny was suave and parked me on the patio, under a huge palm bush with scarlet and orange poinciana scattered like blood against the house. One guest, a chubby Southerner who owned seventeen factories and had a phone in each limousine, answered my question, "What am I doing here? Good God, I don't know! I just picked up the phone and said I'm coming. Once, I came to stay three days and stayed seven weeks. I couldn't move, the jungle rot set in. You're like a sponge down here, *I love it!*"—hoisting his Cuba Libre.

A tanned young man bearing a goblet of cognac rose

dripping from the pool and went indoors.

Danny said, "Tenn cut the *Boom!* script for impact, so that it's all impact and not very convincing because of the shouting. *Boom!* is from *Milk Train*. . . ."

"Even all impact, it's his best movie. What symbols!"

Another tanned young wealthy Southerner plopped into a patio chair with a Cuba Libre, and held it out to me. "I'm not drinking," I said.

Danny said, "Tenn is one of the most kind and moral persons. The kindness is always there, he never takes advantage of anyone—although he gets very perturbed often, and can forgive just as quickly. Whatever it is, he is true to the virtue in himself. With him this is a matter of survival, being true to himself, because it affects his work. He lives for nothing but his work, he's constantly working at his work. I don't think he's ever enjoyed any material things in life. For him, writing is breath! But this island is the end of the road (I don't mean for him), it's where people come to be protected. Finally protected. Of course, he's still very competitive, or used to be, about Broadway, but he hasn't one jealous bone about the accomplishments of others. Ask Bill Inge. He gave Bill a couple of well-placed boosts. But you can ask anyone else he's helped—he's been a fountain of first aid with money. And he's not demanding, not grasping, not avaricious. He's this creature who is shot through with gentleness."

"What debilities," I asked, "do you think Tennessee has risen above to continue in his work?"

"Well, the worst was Frank Merlo's death. He was Tenn's secretary-companion for fourteen years until his death five or six years ago. Tenn has been depressed ever since. But Tenn, writing or living, has this great capacity to idealize, and after the idealizing he has to come in and survive."

"What would you say is his essential virtue?"

"He is working on the virtue of solitariness."

I thought about this and said, "Maybe you can have both."

"Both what?"

"Go fishing by yourself when you need solitude, and enjoy fellowship when you want to join mankind."

"I don't know what you mean by fellowship," he said.

"Neither do I. I'm very bad at it."

Henry Faulkner, a painter, told me, "Tennessee is the most melancholy man on God's green earth. That's what he's overcoming, play after play, as he sits there writing away religiously every morning—for a few hours daily he's overcoming his loneliness. Sending out warnings, distress signals, cries. All that traveling is a geographical escape from it that doesn't work. Every morning he gets crouched right there at the starting line, ready to run to these people in his mind. It's utter loneliness."

"In his new play his painter says he's becoming one with his work and that it's complete pain," I said.

"I understand this, I really do," Henry said. "But also I feel that he's trying to change his wires from Sick to whatever he recognizes as Healthy in himself. He wants to come out of his depression. What really began his violently turning into himself was the time when, in all innocence, he gave two sailors a ride out of Miami and they beat him up and took his watch and car. If you could believe how gentle he is inside you'd realize what a spiritual catastrophe this was for him."

Marie de Marsan, an artist from Paris, told me, "Well, when the devil gets old, he becomes a hermit. Tennessee has risen above the flesh. You know, with age, when the health and appetite weaken, you become spiritual. And the death of Frank Merlo, that penetrated him, every cell. What did he die of? Cancer, I think. They were very close. May I tell you? I went to visit him one morning sometime after Frank died and Tennessee had done this painting for Frank. It was in his bedroom and Tennessee was cold sober. He was very moved and I suppose wanted my opinion. 'Doesn't that look like him, Marie!' And it didn't. But his affection is so intense that to him it is the most beautiful painting in the world. He was cold sober and crying. He saw his friend in that paint, it was merely paint."

At the Southern Cross Hotel I finished reading Gilbert Maxwell's *Tennessee Williams and Friends*, an informal biography. Maxwell, who sometimes thinks of Tennessee as his best friend, tells of Tennessee's occasional bursts of distrust, as when Tenn said to him: "They say you hate me but I don't think so, because God knows I don't think you could say meaner things to my back than you say to my face."

Maxwell replied firmly, "That's for sure . . . I haven't yet joined the backbiting small coterie of hypocrites, envious failures, and bootlicking sycophants who surround you, daddy-o." Despite their intimacy, Maxwell admits that there are "whole areas of Tenn's inner consciousness to which I have never had access." Audrey Wood, the playwright's former agent, who handled some of the larger sums Williams dispensed to friends in need, told Maxwell, "No, it's not just one or two people, by any means. It's a whole group he's helping, and it goes on all the time."

On the afternoon that Reverend Father Joseph LeRoy met Tennessee, they had some scotch and catechism, and next day, bleary from working until three in the morning, Tennessee showed up at the church with his convert brother, Dakin. "Tennessee managed to stay awake while I summarized the Ten Commandments. Then we went into the church and he genuflected and said a prayer. Then he said to me, 'Once upon a time I visited the Cologne Cathedral in Germany. The Grace of God touched me. I never forgot that experience.' . . . Then he lit candles, blessed himself, took out a bill and said, 'For the poor, Father.' That day was the Feast of the Epiphany. . . . Then he asked to be baptized because—although he'd been baptized as a child—he wanted to *feel* it. He professed his faith with his right hand on the Bible, was baptized and knelt at the altar and received communion at evening Mass. . . . Later, when he was flying to Rome, he asked for the rite of the anointing of the sick, and I administered this. He's fearful of his life. After the baptism he impressed me greatly by saying, 'I wanted to have my goodness back.' "

"Well," I said, "his brother Dakin has said that Tennessee is sometimes dismayed by his reputation as being a poet of decadence and death. He sees his plays quite differently—full of affirmation."

"He told me he's finished a new play, *Now and at the Hour of Our Death*."

As I left the Church of St. Mary's Star of the Sea, I looked at the modest altar. Red votive candles burned in banks, and rising high over the altar glowed a Virgin and Child in stained glass of red, blue and yellow against the afternoon sun. I saw Williams kneeling and staring up at the colors. Then I remembered that on the night of his first communion at evening Mass, he'd gone home and had a champagne party.

In 1975 Williams published his memoirs and admitted therein that since 1955 "I have written usually under artificial stimulants, aside from the true stimulant of my deep-rooted need to continue to write." He points to the many plays he's written since 1955 and adds that a list of them "would make you wonder a bit at my ability to continue my work under these debauched conditions." *Memoirs* is full of unclear writing that appears to have had no editing—no one to tell Williams how fogbound his comments about himself sometimes are. Now, of course, his self-admitted egomania will force him to defend every dumb or confused remark he's made in the book. I put it this strongly because young writers across the country will take his memoirs as gospel about what to expect in middle age, which is that artificial stimulants are unavoidable and follow without fail the defeats and buffetings of a writing career—are, indeed, the only way to stem the dimming of energy. He says:

> I could mention many productive and honest writers who went the way of liquor, especially in middle years.
>
> Yet I would, of course, not advise any young writer to elect that way until it is forced upon him, until he cannot continue his work without resorting to stimulants.

He tells that

93

a gifted and handsome young screen writer, seeing me to bed and my bedtime Nembutal, confessed to me that he was able, now, only to write when drinking.

I felt like an older brother, and I said, "You're too young for that, don't take that way yet."

He did not seem to think that there would be offered him another and his handsome face was already beginning to show the coarsening effect of excessive drink.

Then he asks a question which reveals the deep suffering that his stimulants had brought him to:

Is it fair not to offer to writers the same tax-emption for depleted resources that is offered, for instance, to big oil millionaires and steel works and other corporate enterprises which own and run our country?

The suffering came out with an edge of rage when his most recent play, *Clothes for a Summer Hotel*, a "ghost play," closed in Manhattan after a press just as bad as that received eleven years earlier by *In the Bar of a Tokyo Hotel*. This was a play about Zelda and Scott Fitzgerald and included the appearance of Hemingway. It was about Fitzgerald's crackup but lacked a spinal plot. "All I heard was how beautiful it was," he told Michiko Kakutani of the *Times*. "I had some reservations about it, but in the beginning, neither my agent nor my friends said it had problems. People should tell you what is wrong with a play before they rush it into production." Williams was depressed and bitter and angry. "They always say, 'It's not as good as *Streetcar* or *Cat*.' Of course, it's not. At 69, you don't write the kind of play you write at 30. You haven't got the kind of energy you used to have."

Kakutani says, "After a speaking engagement in Tennessee, Mr. Williams retreated to his home in Key West, Fla., to swim and paint and forget. But he couldn't forget. It had been 18 years since his last Broadway success with *Night of the Iguana*, and the fate of *Clothes* confirmed his increasing paranoia that the critics—and, for that matter, the American public—were through with him. He would leave, he decided. He would move to Australia and invent a new life . . . " 'I've been expelled from America, and I'm no longer in the mood to take it. I want to get together the nucleus of a repertory company with one or two American actresses to go down to Australia with me—it's sort of like Custer's last stand.' "*

Byron Dobell, my *Esquire* editor, left the magazine to manage a new book publishing house and had such faith in my writing that he offered me a contract for a new novel if I'd show him sixty pages. I set forth on my first sober book, *The Painter Gabriel*, about a metaphysical painter on the Lower East Side. The novel was written with very few, widely spaced drugs and no alcohol. The two or three pages that were drug-inspired did not survive revision and only a few pot phrases are left, two or three, and one incident: my hero passes his kitchen mirror and sees himself as a distorted Picasso figure. That's the only moment I still recognize as from pot. The whole is more highly charged than I could ever have achieved on drugs. When at last I held in my hand my first published novel, a work whose themes, power and finish beggared all my drug books, from *Prometheus* to *The Body Artist,* I felt gratitude beyond belief for my sobriety. On publication day the novel was praised by John Leonard of the *Times* and my vanity rocketed. I got varnished, wanting to lock into my natural high with a chemical fix that would keep the day radiant for as many seconds as I could suck from its long-awaited hours. I thought I deserved it. What I truly deserved was the resounding treat of being good to myself and not drinking. But the hardest day for a recovering alcoholic is not that of a death in the family but that of great success. A tremendous sweet fell onto my tongue and I wanted

*I include Williams in this book because my writing on him was part of my recovery—the writing itself is (in part) already on record in *Esquire*—and because his own widely published *Memoirs* demand a reply to his attitudes about drugs and writing.

to fix it there forever with a spike of Wild Turkey. Reading my title in the *Times*—it looked stunningly original and fulfilled all my drunken dreams—I felt like Wolfe himself reading the first review of *Look Homeward, Angel* or Byron scanning the first notice of *Childe Harold's Pilgrimage*. I'd been dry over a year and awoke next morning broken in wind, and limped back to my fellowship to acknowledge my relapse. We sat around a big table and I waited like a leper with a spear through my lungs to speak in turn. "My name is Don Newlove and I am an alcoholic and I drank yesterday. I wish I hadn't! But I did. I don't know how many times I've had to sit here and say that. I'd been sober, or dry, for a year. Now I'm one day sober. I feel like I'm carrying a hospital bill as heavy as a Douglas fir up a steep hill. I can't breathe!" And I couldn't. A man raised his hand. "Don't feel guilty," he said, "it's useless." *"But I do!"* "How long are you sober?" "One day." "That's all I'm sober—one day. One day at a time. That's all any of us are sober. We can't be sober for yesterday or for tomorrow. Just for today. So don't make it harder on yourself by carrying an extra weight. Forgive yourself and join the program." And with that a great weight did lift. "But I've had to sit here and admit it so many times." "Why did you drink?" "Well, I got published yesterday after twenty-some years of trying." "No, no, why did you drink?" "I don't know, I wanted to celebrate." "No, no, why are you at this table?" "I'm an alcoholic." "That's why you drank, genius." The room burst into laughter and I got up silently and went into the kitchen to wipe my eyes. I felt welcomed back into the fellowship and no longer was a ghost in a cloud.

By now I'd got serious about alcohol, if not drugs. I wouldn't write on drugs but still pleasured in the sensuality of druggy sex and music and walking about the wide evening undersea with pot colors. I still thought that sobriety meant bottle-fighting, and had many such attitudes which delayed my rebirth. Draining alcohol out of my body was not the be-all of sobriety. It's a step I can't do without, but it's not the first step. The first step is a second thought about my insane goals as a drunk and how my insanity made my life unmanageable. At the moment I came into the fellowship, I'd never had brighter hopes or steadier income and did not think my life unmanageable. But taking away alcohol did not remove the enormous burden of my egomania and sweeping Drunkspearean eagerness to slam the anvil with my *Eroica*. There's nothing wrong with trying to match Beethoven with a novel. It was just hopeless to go about it using the tools of a drunk, even if I wasn't drinking. For example, during my first five years in the fellowship, I wouldn't give another member my telephone number or volunteer to trade numbers. I didn't want some hopelessly sober recoverer phoning me and hearing my pot slur—that damned lisp! Dead giveaway. I wanted to keep my private access to euphoria—beautiful feelings—even though I now saw clearly how pot was a shoehorn into the first drink. I might not drink the night I had pot. But pot reawakened my links to alcohol and perhaps the week following a pot fest would find me slipping into an Eighth Avenue fight bar for a half-price Wild Turkey—who can pass up Wild Turkey at half-price! And so, keeping to myself and being the Lone Wolf of recovery (and still addicted to highs), I also kept a tight grip on my egomania and did not send out shoots as a human being. Oh, be sure I spoke like a prince, a garbled but inspired prince, at my meetings, and cut a memorable figure. How could it be otherwise? My royal fat had outgrown belts, loved suspenders, and hair and beard hung to my waist. My wife had knitted me a huge purple tam like Rembrandt's, all my clothes including sox and underwear were dyed purple, my shirts and jeans were purple and I still had Drunkspeare's purple sunglasses. When I went to a meeting, I brought two big pipes, pipe cleaners, a reamer, two or three tobaccos, cigarettes, a lighter and a notepad for my brilliancies and they would be arranged before me on the table like juju fetishes showing my sobriety. I had clearly bent my alcoholism into tobacco. I shone like a purple Pope. My idea for all this was that I was pysching myself into being spiritually active in my writing, and purple was the hue

97

of those divinely appointed figures through whom God spoke. How could the fairly sane author of *The Painter Gabriel* still be so close to the loony-bin? Because I was not ready for deflation at depth of my Drunkspearean ego. Not ready for sanity (drunks can write shrewdly in their insanity). And despite attendance, not ready to join the fellowship. I was a hopeless alcoholic and didn't know it—not yet, not yet. My little powder drunk with a drug capsule? My midnight pot flights with Scriabin? I could handle them. For five years in the fellowship, I handled an insane, unmanageable life masked with a smile of Arthurian virtue, with the smarts of my research, and at the table or on my feet speaking before groups I arose masked with the eloquence of a reformed angel. And *I* believed it too! In my silvertongued cunning I'd give you the poetry of the ages—my rapturous sobriety—then go home to my stash. But *how* could I be so double-minded? It took a tank car of self-deceit. Yet sometimes I'd derail, choke up, turn purple, stammer, flub and lisp for fifteen or twenty minutes, the bilge so high-flown even I couldn't speak it. Then, going home, I'd sigh to my wife, "This has been the most moving night of my life. I've never before touched a group that deeply. You could hear a pin drop!" I suspect now they were wondering if I'd fall dead in my changing agonies.

Dobell asked for another novel and I set forth on one which I thought would contrast the rival philosophies of Tolstoy and Dostoievsky, or Leo and Fyodor, a pair of genius brothers raised in a little upstate New York town. Ha ha ha—do you hear a familiar whisper behind this inspiration? My shadow self, still dreaming his colossal dreams. I don't have to drink to be Drunkspeare. Somewhere in my old publisher's office may lie the first plot outline by which I received a modest advance for fashioning this whale. It was gigantic, a baggy-pants Russian monster for America, hoping to rival Mailer's epic announced in *Advertisements for Myself*:

. . . the book will be fired to its fuse by the rumor that once I pointed to the farthest fence and said that within ten years I would try to hit the longest ball ever to go up into the accelerated hurricane air of our American letters.

There was a dream for Drunkspeare to conjure with, and of course there's always plenty of room at the top for a Proust *and* a Joyce. Contract signed for a novel projected at 900 pages, I froze—and for three months failed to write the first word. Many notes, no beginning, just paralyzing ambition.

At last I fell in love with my wife Jackie. Too bad for me, she'd started going the other way. So I swore off pot and devoted myself to her for six months, the strongest commitment I could muster. And I wanted this novel to be drug-free. For three months I sat around my fellowship table and complained of my fears and paralysis, hinting heavily that perhaps only one night on pot was what I needed to bust out of this writing block. I'd explain carefully that my method of writing was to write a first draft in longhand, type that up, correct and retype it from start to finish, then again correct and totally retype it. Since the novel was set at NINE HUNDRED PAGES, this meant that when done I'd have filled THIRTY-SIX HUNDRED PAGES with my writing. This was daunting. The idea that I would have to fill 3600 pages with my imagination was now a black mountain of work that had kept me stoned with weakness for three months. I wooed my wife but did little else. My wife, meanwhile, found me drug-free almost too weird to live with. I wasn't writing but somehow she'd lost her purpose in living with me. She began to dislike being touched, turned her face when I kissed her, and endured lovemaking with little enjoyment. Who was this health-minded android with empty blue eyes walking around our apartment? It was as if I'd had the Swedish operation for Siamese twins and been unjoined from my drunken brother. One evening at the fellowship table, after I'd again complained and described the deflation of my writing spirit, somebody said a recovery slogan which I'd heard for years now—and only on this night did it sink in. Divine repetition is for slow learners like me. This dumb phrase suddenly filled me with light. It was: One Day at a Time. Black waters boiled, a thrilling berg broached the lid of my unconscious, my novel churned heavenward before me. To write it I had only to write one word at a time, one phrase at a time, one clause at a time, one sentence at a time, one paragraph at a time, one page at a time, one day at a time—and if I wrote four pages a day I'd be done in three years. The magnitude of the results of this simpleminded approach to boating my white whale sent me home like a shot after the meeting and I jumped at the diningroom table with a blank sheet and began. First I threw out Tolstoy and Dostoievsky and left just Leo and Theodore (Fyodor), then because I lived with a twin I made them twins, and feeling the tug of Drunkspeare toward mucking it up with superfantastico grandiosity, made them blood-joined Siamese twins. If I had known the problems before me, I'd have frozen again. No one had ever written a serious novel about Siamese twins. I was starting from ground zero without a model. Four years later, I finished the first published versions of my twin novels *Leo & Theodore* and *The Drunks*. The first volume as I worked one day at a time, was published within two years of my sitting at the table. The first draft was written drug-free, and the second and third. Then I quavered. Was it really imaginative enough? I sat staring at *Leo & Theodore*. Wasn't an even richer, *Parsifal*-like brilliance possible? *More light?* I decided to read through the entire manuscript on pot. Visited my old pusher Doctor Sunshine and returned toasted and well-stocked for the big read. The first page fell apart. Too many words! My God, this is very dull. You've got to compress down to the tightest telegraphic style that will still carry the life of the sentence. I spent three months carrying out this pot inspiration I'd locked into, but not smoking pot again and without alcohol. The published volume was light-filled to bursting, enormously lively, and for most readers unreadable without great attention to every syllable. If the reader tried to skim even one page, he'd fall asleep. But I'd mastered this style and kept it up through *The*

Drunks, which was even harder to read and unskimmable. Four years after *The Drunks* came out, Robert Wyatt of Avon Books offered to republish the two novels in one paperback. With joy I set to and loosened the telegraphic style with several thousand corrections, titled the work *Sweet Adversity* and at last saw in print the drug-free novel about alcohol that sprang from my life's earliest memory—my father dipping a kitchen match into a shot of whiskey and raising it out still burning—

> They see the flame on their father's glass, the alcohol a naked virgin, dancing, burning in a shameless blue frenzy.

Jackie left me and flew to Europe as I finished *Leo & Theodore* and took a deep breath to begin *The Drunks*. We said goodbye at an elevated train turnstile near our apartment at Jerome and Shakespeare Avenues in the Bronx (St. Jerome, of course, first translated the Scriptures into the Vulgate, and so Drunkspeare thought this the luckiest writer's address in the States)—her birdbright blue eyes asked if she should stay, but she knew she was going and she did. Always tissuing the instant, even then. We've remained very fond friends and last made love that same day, as my new girlfriend was getting ready to move in later in the afternoon, which Jackie knew. She also knew I was never at a loss for hypocrisy in the course of a fast satisfaction. But I was winging toward my last drink.

My new roommate, Bonnie, was twenty, a writer-painter (she'd written five novels already), and still violently adolescent. She lived with me for two years, until I was forty-four, and as a gentleman I always introduced her as my fiancée. She went to fellowship meetings with me. My few friends around the table, those whose names had finally been dinned into me after five years, made every effort to consider me sober but something about slim little Bonnie and me looked instantly awry. Her blonde hair was very long but mine longer and I still was the Purple Pope (lavender underwear, too). My eyes were odd: the force of my double-dealing had driven them half out of their sockets, like a toy bulldog's, and walleyed. Weird to catch

101

sight of my pot-swacked hero in the bathroom mirror and find his eyes rolling away from each other. When I laid out my pot-smoking paraphernalia on the livingroom table, Bonnie's face would blow up with blood and her lips bloat with disbelief and disgust. I felt swell, really on top, but you only had to look and the thought would occur, That guy just *can't* be sober. As a sop to sobriety, I gave up cigarettes.

I was invited, fee-paid, to speak at the University of Florida at Gainesville and flew down alone,—no, not quite . . . The Writer Drunkspeare, in his last hairy phosphorescence, joined me. The drug arias of *The Painter Gabriel* went before me and after the reading—which opened with two unaccompanied horn solos by me, "Cornet Chop Suey" and "Struttin' with Some Barbecue"—a table was proudly revealed with unopened variety liquors worth $150, as my host Dick Benoit made clear. Moral courage failed me, for a moment, but I went outdoors, blew a joint and returned to coast through the evening dry. Next day, alone at the Benoits' and practicing my horn, I found a bottle of Strawberry Hill wine opened in the icebox. I'd never had this high-schoolers' special, a drink I equated with Girl Scout cookies, and having spurned the gorgeous booze heaped before me the night before, I thought I could handle without fear one sip of this tasty new crock of sweets that had appeared on the market since I joined the fellowship. All my horrors, black-bordered hangovers, and endless disasters vanished from memory, and I unscrewed the top and took my lone sip of kid stuff. *Agh!* I cried out as electricity shot up the backs of my legs. Within fifteen minutes I was at the state shop a block away buying a fifth of Jack Daniel and soon settled into a dim powderblue cocktail lounge ordering ice and a setup, my booze on the table, and sucking flavorously at cigarettes through bourbon fumes. *My God, this is living.*

I floated across Florida to visit my mother before going home, we drank late, and in the morning I stiff-legged my body into the kitchen and faced a nearly full backup bottle on the sink counter. I was two hundred and fifty pounds of fine-sliced ham still sticking into human form. I poured two ounces of Ethyl into a waterglass and drained it. The booze bloomed through my shoulders, then fell like deathsalts through my body. Every cell was stunned, my brain a gnarled fist of smoke. Death wavered within me like a second body. Self-insult and humiliation could go no deeper. I'd hit bottom.

"That was my last drink," I said to my mother.

And it has been.

I flew back to my fellowship, trembling, shamed to the core, and carried my unadmitted relapse like a black weight from meeting to meeting, until I'd been sober ninety days. Then I told my fellowship sponsor. "Oh, I knew that," he said, "but you should've told me anyway, genius. It's stupid to suffer guilt like that. Whattaya think I'm here for? Why do I bother to love you and give you the best fucking care you'll ever know? Agh, sometimes you make me sick. Anyway I'm glad ya told me. You may make this program yet. *If* you follow one simple but profound rule: Don't drink and go to meetings. Got that, lamebrain?"

My poet friend whom I'd followed into the program after he'd visited me in my apartment five years earlier drove up from Pennsylvania for a visit, and I told him of my Florida relapse. Face of granite, utterly unmoved, he stared at me and rasped, "When are you going to join the fellowship, Don?"

That rasp drew blood. "I thought I was *in* the fellowship!"

"You call that fellowship?" His glittering right pupil burst with disdain. "Shit, I call it tourism."

"I feel awful."

"Letting us all down, year after year after year? *Fellowship?*"

"Well, I'm gonna do better!" I began crying.

"Why don't you get off your ass and get active? Get your feet wet in sobriety?"

"Well, I'd—I'd—I'd been planning to."

"No weaseling half-measures, Don. I mean body and soul."

"*Ohhh!*" I was flowing.

"When are you going to be ready? When can we expect *the miracle?*"

"*I'M READY!*"

"Fine. 'Nuff said," he said, looking about. "Christ, do I need this meeting."

Sobering up at last was as dramatic as watching grass grow in heaven. Every three months or so I'd look back and find a deeper shade of green now enriching my spirit. All my old self-holiness dropped away, as did my beard and ponytail and purple raiment. When I walked out of the barber shop, looking (and feeling!) ten years younger, my voice also had dropped from strangled hysteric tenor to mild baritone: I no longer had Drunkspeare to defend. With all my heart, I bent to my recovery. I began an inventory, as suggested by the program, of all my faults and virtues—a fearless and searching inventory—and when I finally admitted this inventory to my Higher Power and to my sponsor, I no longer had many of my old guilts to suck on and pore over or ignore, as I saw fit, and I had a better grasp of my strengths. Deep in the pit of me lay one atom of hope that suggested I might not be an iron-skinned, hopeless alcoholic. Daily, I stood before the judge, and hoped. Alcohol was a power greater than myself—how well I knew!—a giant raging about the countryside. I'd stay far away from his haunts and not get into bottle-fighting, sure death, knowing I would tire at last if he leaned hard on me. Be sensible, Don, don't tempt or romance him. He can have an overwhelming smile when he offers the first ounce and all your fears and old humiliations nod off into slumber. Going by figures, only one out of twenty victims achieves lasting re-covery. You've recovered many times, Don, let's try for *lasting* recovery, one day at a time. Be careful, don't get hungry, angry, lonely or tired, that's when he comes scratching at your window. That's when he rises up and casts a black shadow, hoping to awaken Drunkspeare and all your old feelings toward yourself, the hopeless overcast, sarcasm, sentimental heartbreak, shrivel you dry and get *him* dancing on the grapes, all squushy and drunk—remember those wonderful days, wailing on the linoleum? All your old floors are waiting for you, Don, they'd love to move here. But my God, I'd think, look at the world, the sheer tragedy and horror—maybe sobriety is all for nothing. Maybe you've been fed horseshit and this isn't a disease—and you *can* handle it. And night falls, and wheezing sighs rise, as Giant Despair whispers on: "Not a disease, not a disease!" "I don't care, I have it." "That's nonsense." "Good God, If *I* don't have it, who does?" "But what about the Bomb, the war dead everywhere, cancer, crime in the streets and murder without end? Surely an honest hopelessness is better than lies and sugarwater." "Sobriety is not harder on me than I've already been on myself." But even if I were the ultimate victim of all diseases and ills, getting drunk would only add one more hardship and take none away. In the morning I'd be right back facing a burglarized apartment, or thoughts of the Bomb and the war dead, but with a hangover and less spirit than nature endowed me with. Anyway, I don't project doom and misery. Today is terrific and I live one day at a time. Today is all I have any power over. I have friends who faced cancer sober and died in utter serenity, saying they were "Just fine." With luck, I'll have that choice. If I die sober, I'll have hit out of the park the longest ball I was born to hit, the one nature meant me to hit when it first fashioned me as a drunk. Nature wants me sober. It loves strength, that why it makes most strong those places that heal—broken spirits, especially—and makes them more unbreakable than when they were tested and first broke. Rebirth tempers you with strength you never had before. I think hopelessness is *dis*honest and sentimental. Yesterday (as I write this) I visited my wife Nancy's 94-year-old Armenian father in a nursing home where he lies with illnesses and injuries he keeps overcoming one at a time—a clear-minded man not able to meet his basic physical needs beyond lifting a spoon. His dignity would temper a president. He absorbs broken hips, strokes, sores, blindness, and lives alone in the dark with his colostomy bag and unwavering faith in the goodness of life—he's had that bag in his anus since surviving rectal cancer ten years ago. His wife died thirty-five years ago. He's been waiting to see her again, and now more than ever is in deep darkness as he lives on day after day, night after night. He wants her to walk into his bedroom and lead him out. And yet he lives on, year after year. Who am I with my puppy piss about art and pining to write great books, who am I to stand here in my full health pissing up a rope about my alcohol habit, when this man says to me every morning, "Hello, darling! Good to see you! Is that my Donald? Sit and talk to me, I love to hear your voice." "Christ, are you still here, Dad?" "Ha ha ha!—*that's the voice.* Read to me, darling, something you're writing." "Okay, this is from my new book about my drinking career." "Love it! I knew a lot of good fellows who died of it. I'll tell you sometime and you can put it in." "Okay, Dad. Were they writers?" "Ha ha ha, they weren't even readers!" "Well, we'll see. This is about the death of my father—" "Was he an alcoholic?" "Who am I to say? But he sure shouldn't have been drinking with diabetes and TB. 'My father died on a windy street corner in Erie'—this won't depress you?" "Wonderful! You never depress me, darling. Go on, I'm all ears."

And he counts every breath in the dark, waiting for her fingers to slip into his. "Come along, Tom, I'm here." "*Darling!*"

I was a little strengthened by doing my fearful inventory (there were brute acts I'd hide even from my analyst), felt better after reading it over with my fellowship sponsor and privately admitting it was the best I could do for the time being. My greatest difficulty was entertaining some thought of a Higher Power I might speak to in my heart. All my saints were dead drunks, aside from some composers who had direct access to heaven. The heavens of music were greater assurance to me of a Divine Spirit than words in print. Prayers had power to move me, such as the verse from the Book of Common Prayer spoken for burials at sea. There was no holding back the power of that prayer. Sometimes a face, my wife's, a friend's, or one I saw at a meeting, would light up from within and shock me with a sense of God moving through flesh. I had mainly, of course, dabbled in Better Gods Through Chemistry and was a one-hundred-proof pantheist. Skies in their infinitudes, bodies of water, countrysides and hills, I was always eager for the big picture and found God irresistible in His greater works. Pot and booze broke down the checks of logic and allowed me to feel what Stone Agers experienced naturally. I also had a spiritual eye for the small in nature. I drew the line at Fundamentalism, the truth of the Scriptures, Bible miracles, virgin birth, resurrection of the body in *any* religion, and I was skeptical of the Crucifixion. But since I had just been through a crucifixion (a little one, for sure, but very important to me), and had seen many friends less lucky die of my very illness, whose agent was a two-faced Judas chemical that kissed as it killed, I was ready to accept the Crucifixion as a spiritual mystery, and most Christian miracles as metaphors for the uses of adversity. I no longer cared about historical fact, but only about the Wind that blew through me. If it uplifted, it was good. One evening on Fourteenth Street I broke open my horn case and played the lead on "What a Friend We Have in Jesus" with a Salvation Army band. I was psyching myself for touching my unadmitted Higher Power and for three months a terrific cloud built in me, so that everywhere I turned I saw signs and warnings, heard an inner whisper, and sighed under an avalanche of coincidences. I could take just so many coincidences before their pull became tidal. One afternoon, going down the hall from my kitchen to my study, my feet were swept back, I landed on my knees as if scythed, and found myself in a cloudburst of prayer. I hobbled into my bedroom and went on praying beside the bed, sobbing without stop. After that I felt compelled to go to my typewriter and send a batch of letters to people I felt I'd injured while drinking. Then I decided to return all my stolen books and records to the Donnell Library in midManhattan, which I did and got a staggering fine. But as I explained to the head librarian, a Chinese lady, that I was an alcoholic and intent on making restitution, that I'd have to pay it off in installments— this was a ten-year harvest of fines for hundreds of books and records—we dickered about my weekly payment until, to avoid bookkeeping costs, she lumped it all into one payment of fifteen dollars, which I paid without pausing—and then I raced outdoors, leaving her with my boxes of sins. On the street I was unhappy that I had not returned the books and records earlier in my sobriety, rather than having faced their guilty spines for so long in my living room.

That night in bed I faced my last embarrassment with prayer. My trouble had always been that I felt like a fake when praying, and had been too self-aware for a natural flow of thoughts. I'd no sooner get on my knees than I'd blush at the dumbness of what I was doing. I prided myself for my brains, detested sentimentality, was a badger for logic, a perfectionist about everything, and these attitudes stiffened as I tried to speak simply to a Higher Being I sensed was guiding me. I could not escape *me*. So I got into bed, having said the Lord's Prayer, and tossed about in my failure. My sponsor's face rose before me and I said Bless Emery. Another face from the fellowship table arose. I said Bless Tom. Then another. Bless Jeff. Bless Helene. Bless Jack. Bless Euell. And I went around the table, blessing each member by name. Then I blessed my dead friends. My mother and sister and each family member, all the members of my wives' families. Like mushrooms more faces popped up demanding blessing, and I was soon into members at several fellowship meetings. The faces were backing up, but I named each one in a blessing. At least a half hour had gone by of intense blessing and I was nowhere near exhausted of friends. I've got to stop this and get to sleep, I gotta get up in the morning! But the faces poured in unstoppably and I was too fearful to leave anyone out who asked. And yet the very plenitude of faces kept me so gladdened at the sight of each rounded, smiling head with its eyes looking into me that I lay tearstained with openhearted prayer, no mask, no personality, only a direct pipeline of blessings from my Higher Power to my friends in the fellowship and to my family and doctor and even the dead, my dead father and dead stepfathers, who surely needed a good word, my sister's dead baby Charlie, my friends in the Marines and Air Force, Paul and his wife Marian, my childhood friends, my old fellow reporters on the *Sun*, my friends in publishing and reviewing, on and on and on, you can't withhold a blessing if someone smiles at you in a dream of prayer.

This kind of secret praying had the disquieting effect of making everyone look like an angel, or flesh-spirit. Especially when smiling directly at me, and then each would be a suffering angel plunged into flesh. Beclouded girls, one stalked by violence and kept in fear, another beset by brain cancer (we'd been lovers) and dying, both recovering drunks, struck me as struggling angels, or spirits being tempered. I saw ideal nature in human form, resisting the easy despair of alcohol and becoming brainier and winged with sobriety. At fellowship meetings the people of my prayers swam about me with intense familiarity, a spirit-shine in flesh, lips, lighted eyes. I saw gesturing skeletons and their musculature and hair and was not sad that we were resisting disease, no matter that life passed from these bones. Even if there is no life to come, it is still better to live this life at full light than dimmed by drugs. I loved my friends' desire to be sober. My spirit sang to see them in their health. I loved our sociality, even if we were mere moths of the century. Nonetheless, I began to lose my humor or head for small talk and jokes, forever aware of deep-running currents passing through us. People laughed or smiled with happiness that I saw as a tragic, earnest energy overcoming the darkness that is always near. Meetings had a nimbus over the table and members. At my main meeting, the table we sat at appeared to float on amber light after an hour or so and for the last half hour a running, leaping fire knotted the faces into a circle of human light that was unearthly in its work of purifying these happy, smiling damaged people: they made the light and, unaware, sat in its cleansing. My being took on an edge and a rasp I'd never known, tempered by faces that did not know their own heat. This tragic sense stayed with me for three years as I became a Stalinist about recovery and wrote *The Drunks*. It was the most intense period of my life. Throughout I made coffee weekly for my main meeting, answered phones every Saturday morning at the office to which drunks phone in for help, traded names and phone numbers with fellow recoverers and *made return calls*, was chairman of two meetings, spoke hundreds of times and at hospitals and prisons, carted the sick to drying out farms, sponsored dozens of drunks through their first year of recovery and afterward, devoted myself to the formal program of our fellowship and read its literature, wrote articles for our world magazine, worked for free at our central office, went on housecalls, to funerals, to visit members in hospitals, held meetings for shut-ins, socialized after meetings at coffee shops, and "got off my ass and got active." I found myself in a fellowship of rounded beings with lives flowing out of them, people who did not want to die on the kitchen floor or wrapped around phone poles or stepping out into traffic on the red light. They were responsible for me and I was responsible for them, one man at a time, and as many as still would allow me a full life of my own. The miracle was that the more I helped the more time I had. I did not have time to drink or think about drugs for myself. I was light as some balsawood man released from the darkest ocean trench and rising through miles of relaxing pressure toward radium daylight. I was my own breakthrough novel. When I listened to the earthpeople with their problems, folks with no program or fellowship of recovery like mine, I thought I was hearing Martians. Perhaps they could have a rebirth renting pews or buying votive candles, but I saw only endless misery for them as they muddled and stewed, mistrusting each other, timid in hope, not daring, not great-hearted, fearful in their office, sick-spirited, dying on their feet, not happy at all to be tested with illness and shaken into new life. But that was my Stalinist period, and I've mellowed. Perhaps I was angry with myself for having resisted those living handshakes for five years in the fellowship. And all my talk about prayer doesn't make me a saint. I could be drunk and dying tomorrow. *Not* today, it's very unlikely today, I've chosen not to drink today, the only day I have real control over.

My fellowship remains nameless here because its anonymity and the anonymity of its members is a priceless spiritual support offered to the recoverer, who may join and know his secret is safe. Many alcoholics are secret drinkers, or think no one knows they're alcoholics. Despite every ravage I suffered, neither I nor my friends thought I was an alcoholic— even after I joined the fellowship!—only my poet friend, an admitted alcoholic, who thought I was "hopeless." I admitted to a drinking problem, hoped to return to alcohol once I'd "recovered," had no idea that lasting recovery is forever—or it's not lasting, is it, it's just tourism. There is a stigma to alcoholism not seen with any other disease. It says, if you're a victim, you have poor moral fibre, a weakness that makes you a victim by choice. This shows ignorance. When alcohol chooses *you*, you drink because you drink. What's unique about alcoholism is that it's the only disease where recovery is possible once you admit you're hopelessly ill. You must hit your personal bottom of hopelessness, where you recognize you can't stop by yourself. No two bottoms are the same. I was never hospitalized. Many less violently ill than I were. I should have been, but was too dumb to know better, and lay in bed hallucinating when I could have had a fear-vanishing vitamin shot and medical help. I thought it noble to suffer self-reliantly, and did not want to be a "certified" alcoholic at Bellevue. I'll add that when a member breaks his anonymity, thoughtlessly, it may frighten some fearful soul from joining, someone sensitive about being known as a problem drinker, or afraid of his family members finding out, or his boss, or perhaps he lives in a small town, or is a doctor—what surgeon could face public exposure as a drunk? Many professionals face similar fears. Before I got sober, I feared that public knowledge that I was a recovering alcoholic would dim my chances as a writer, perhaps even lend me a leprous cast among my writing peers, the scarlet label SOBER stamped on my brow. "You mean he doesn't drink *ever*? That must have an awful effect on his writing, don't you think?" Oh, I would miss all the publishers' lunches and book parties! Stand out like an idiot with my sparkling water and lime! Pale, palsied and tongue-tied! Ha ha, I enjoy those parties more than anyone—I'm really *there* and not lisping away in a fog.

Anyway, nobody cares if I'm drinking, they're more interested in their own. Still, a second reason my fellowship stays nameless here is that if I identify myself with it, I put it and myself in an uncomfortable position should I have a relapse that's noted publicly. Lastly, I don't want to make money off our fellowship of the Sun, which has not only saved my life but given me the freedom and light to live it. I'd hardly want to capitalize on this killer disease, or the fellowship that gives eyes to the fatally benighted, then makes powerhouses out of fear-ridden spirits groping through a baffling, cunning, insidious fog. I too was a fogbound honest man who used to drink warm piss and think I was happy. Now I have all this, a state Drunkspeare could never have earned if he'd written through all eternity and sold every work. Maybe my greater life doesn't lie in print but in direct access to the feeble in spirit. What can I say about those helping hands that lifted me from death and squared me face-to-face with Giant Despair? Praise them— how? They were anonymous.

"Don't take me for a fast learner, for God's sake," I told Gil Orlovitz at my favorite fellowship meeting when he asked me about alcohol and writing. "They *don't* mix!"

I knew him as the author of *Milkbottle H*, an unreadably poetic art novel (sound familiar?) about his Philadelphia childhood. He wasn't famous. His reputation was more secure in England, he told me, where his second novel had also appeared to acclaim. I like his poems much more than his fiction—he thought of himself as a poet. A giant in a hanging but respectable suit, listening hard (casual superhuman intensity) but always replying from his private wrinkle in the world, he was distinguished, dark, stooped, and sallow with a high leaden beard he shaved nearly to his eyes. Gnawing a cigarette and dragging until his eyes squinched, he told me about black decades of paralyzing anxiety, nameless, soul-sick fear which had at last crippled him and left him with a spine-deep, daily uselessness that finally laid him in a pauper's grave in Hart Island city cemetery.

He had choices to make about sobering up, and his choices were almost uniformly deadly. He made vague gestures toward attending many more meetings; dried out for a few months on a drying out farm; went on welfare. But he was on a daily maintenance of "five martinis"—handcrafted, of course, and how many ounces? Large hands hanging with coffee and butt, forehead heavily lined with fog, he told me seriously about cutting down. It's hard for one Drunkspeare to listen to another's chemicasting silently, but I would, then suggest that recovering means Don't Drink and Go to Meetings. He preferred the lone wolf role—his individuality was threatened rather than liberated by fellowship. "Oh?" I said, "I think you can have both." It was his booze that was threatened, not his individuality—but I avoid argument with active drinkers, rely on hopeful talk and power of example. Guide, don't push, I warn that hewer and doer in me.

Later, I visited him at Roosevelt Hospital's drying out ward. A dismal room but Gil seemed comfortable, even smiling, grateful for the visit. Boy, he was a tall sonofagun, even in the alky ward's paper slippers—lank dark hair and intense brown eyes, always smiling with self-absorbed humor, self-concern, fear, self-hatred, paralyzing anger with himself (hidden beneath his constant, defensive soft laugh), the smile of a tall, strong intellectual wiped out down to his anus by remorse and guilt.

Nobody claimed his body soon after when he collapsed on West 108th Street and never regained consciousness.

His reasons for drinking were the usual cop-outs: "chronic insomnia," anxiety, separation from family, writer's block, loneliness, even cigarettes (five packs a day)—all fakes, all self-deceits that allowed him one more day on his maintenance "five" martinis. No matter how forcefully I pricked his alibis (when I couldn't control myself), the fog and quicksand rolled right back in. The pivot of his rationale was that being a writer largely unrecognized in his own country justified his self-destruction. "John Berryman's complaint," I'd say (Berryman had written a book about his own drying out farms and Alcoholics Anonymous meetings), "is that the poet 'equips himself, and he's vulnerable, and in our society he gets no support.' My heart sinks at such crosseyed fingerpointing, Gil. Don't make society or the literary community responsible for your fucking boozing, please. Try hard, don't do it."

"Maybe you're right." But the eyes misted.

One summer night I drove Gil home from an extraordinarily powerful meeting of our fellowship. He was elated. Just back from six weeks at a fairly stiff drying out farm and now eight weeks dry. It'd happened at last—his black anxiety had lifted! First time since adolescence. His relief was terrific, a new breath filled him. And filled me—here was hope at last. Even he tied the lifting of his eternal anxiety to the taking away of alcohol and the inspiration of fellowship. As he hunched in my Bug, a wonderful light was filling those great black shining eyes, the first hint that by being honest with himself an indescribable confidence was being born. Not the confidence of "my prose will last forever" but the faith from a searching and fearless look at his alibis.

It was a great drive through Central Park and so I was doubly flattened a few weeks later when, haggard, smiling defensively, he extolled to me his new five-martini dike system for holding back his disease and "functioning." His anxiety had returned full force but he was writing two lines of poetry daily. "Gil," I suggested, "two lines a day despite gin, not because of it." (Divine repetition! so necessary.) No, if he could quit smoking first, then he could quit drinking. If his anxiety would lift again . . . "But I *am* getting my two lines a day, thank God."

So he valued his life at two lines a day and carried a mountain of darkness. Gloom-fighting wherever he went (and losing), nervous, protective of his habit, hostile to any fresh air upon his self-absorption. "I can handle it," he assured me, smiling, his three-day beard like nails.

Still, I was hopeful. I'd said the same things myself. If Gil wanted to hole up with his pen in his mouth and without our fellowship, if he wasn't ready, we'd wait him out until he hit bottom and was teachable. It's the hardest job in the world, as hard as stopping yourself, to let a friend drink himself to his bottom before he asks for help.

But his bottom fell through.

thirst Artist

Part Two

Little Dreamland

Corroded as a Spad on a movie lot . . .
—Jack McManis

I needed gods to steer by and keep me spellbound.

Great slaking thirst artists, masters made strong by hearts of alcohol, bolting out pages of genius but overwhelmingly haunted. Drink was their sign, but if not drink mere madness would do. Poe, Baudelaire, Céline, Artaud, overflowingly deranged angels of the highest order of light. I wanted plenty, superfluity, imagination in excess. Bittersweet torment to match my own, brimming and running over.

I speak for those fabled writing drunks whose careers I'm about to sketch, and those gents sit right here listening. The spirit is moving. Our table floats. Tonight we drink, but of a different spirit as we look back, cool and apart from works gone by. I'm moved by much this table has done, if not its booze triumphs. Divine repetition—most good work done on drink is despite drink, not because of it, with drink only adding one more fog between desire and fulfillment. That's my view.

One of our friends tonight is Edwin Arlington Robinson, the poet of hopeless hope. He never drank before six in the evening on work days, and was almost speechlessly shy unless drinking. He couldn't make friends. And his poems are about dead men singing in the sun, ashes and echoes and twilight on ruins, brown, thin leaves that skip with a freezing whisper and words out of the past like dead, remembered footsteps on old floors. A dreary, lonely, gloomy, flat, sad, shadowy, lorn and hopeless poet who spent four or five decades describing cloudbanks of woe. What melancholy! Don't get angry if I laugh at a sad poet—he *hung* onto his illness, squeezed it masterfully, enshrined it, died of it after going poor and unrecognized into middle age. I'm not flogging him. But his gift ran out and now oblivion has a fast grip on the bulk of his work. His suicide poems are still admired for their skill and irony, and some other poems. But his illness was vicious and killing, and stuffed him with love of despair—this table's community property—until he spent his last decades thoughtfully page-grinding and weighing his tears. For him, alcohol was death around the clock. Worse—a half-death in greylight.

Death isn't easy to give up. We all know how he felt sipping away at it, verse after verse. And we know it more strongly some days than others, when the romance floods back with a knockout whiff of orangeblossom scotch, or we go up on Wagner, thoughts of our days as Tristan and writing our *Romeo and Juliets*, and suddenly we're nose to nose with new products that spear us with lust: half-gallon whisky bottles (now that bottle might stay potent for two or three hours), tasty sweets for high-schoolers, flavorous new concoctions in the Sunday ads—a Swiss or Dutch chocolate-cherry gin in a porcelain bottle (my sweet tooth throbs), page after page of salted margueritas and noble colossi of Stolichnaya vodka, gigantic scotch bottles towering over the New York skyline, brandies shown in luscious printer's inks, rums and cold-steamed beers that almost pour out of the pictures, images dense with homefeelings for the old lies, taste-memories that dry the palate with past drinking joys (ha!), at the Broadmoor lounge in Colorado Springs, the iced martinis at Harry's in Venice, awful fundadors and anisettes in Barcelona, my cold wineskin of marsala through Italy, morning gin and lime in London, stout in pubs, cold, strong Mexican beers, ales at McSorley's, May wine in Yorkville and Oktoberfest bocks—every Sunday tidal nostalgia pouring from the *Times* magazine section. And I forget the convulsions on the kitchen linoleum, breakfast tablespoons of Tabasco, the trots and losses fade far away and the dream rolls back and the poetry of the unfulfilled alcoholic high no wings can reach. Death fades and we lap up the old lies and feel some blessing just at our fingertips if we'll . . . . take that first drink. One drink will do it! give me back all my liquid bullets through the brain, and leave me thrice-filled, brimming over, *Times*worthy, fulfilled. Death isn't an easy daydream to kick, not as you sit gripping your double-strength gin highball and the long African sundown widens over the plains in blue-green twilight, or wherever your *Times* reverie takes place. Christ, turn the page!

Each morning while he shaved Robinson faced that same robot stare we all faced. But the disease can't take away his very real achievements. It did take away mighty tracts out of what more he might have accomplished, it left an immensely shortened shelf of first-rate work. It gave to each man at this table bouts of madness, sickness, suicidal grief, and gradual darkening of talent. We forgive ourselves the horrors the disease drove us to. Our best pages will live, and time do what it will with the rest.

Of all the writers here (and he's English), only one thought his genius sprang from drink. Despite this, his life shows that his only strong work was done while sober; or rather *dry*—he was never really sober, never freed. Malcolm Lowry used drink to avoid writing. Every drunk meant a vacation from work and from meeting (or failing) the grand standards he set himself. First drafts dishearten when they fail to match our best pages already in print: page by page, we compete endlessly with our own works and long for the big spirit-boost that assures us we are still fully empowered. He ground away all his adult life at an ambitious novel series, and it fizzled out. His masterpiece *Under the Volcano* is a weddingcake of rarified description and Boschlike detail, but it's only fitfully on fire. This man's will-to-drink was inhuman, stunning, reckless beyond belief, a downhill, terrified race to the Pit. By a bit of mental mischief, he allowed himself to believe that he would find heaven and serenity in his hell of despair. He bolted from do-gooders who'd want to sober him up. An unusual drunk, very crafty, he could hide like a fox in a blind stupor, then next day repeat every word he'd overheard. But he *looked* five times drunker than is humanly possible. An awesome boozer, and later in life a raving barfighter. At the last any golden relief from the first lift of alcohol was short-lived and followed by bursts of tears, insanity, self-loathing, remorse, and cutting guilt.

Monumental self-absorption (he was the most interesting person he'd ever met), inability to show love, lockjaw timidity, impotence, and a need to complicate his work past all narrative interest. But he was a charmer!—to make up for his endless misdeeds. One night he's a murderous fiend earnestly strangling his wife . . . and soon they're planning a trip like lovebirds. Sometimes he clears up without warning and becomes terrifyingly pleasant company, wise, witty, meltingly beautiful, a good carpenter, ardent swimmer, writing zealot, a joy to know and a sweetheart to his wife. Then comes the first drink again, a harmless beer, wine with dinner. . . .

His wife sticks. Falling into despair when she tries to match his drinking. Enabling him to continue his downward plunge. Sometimes she commits him.

One time he undergoes barbaric "aversion treatments" in

an English hospital. He's isolated in a tiny cell with a red bulb, given shots of apomorphine to induce nausea and vomiting, then given all the alcohol he wants, with very little food or water. The idea is that he'll learn to throw up at the thought of alcohol. Most drunks can take this cell for only five days at best. He lasts twenty-one, then breaks out of the hospital, goes on a forty-eight-hour binge, and returns roaring and very pleased with himself. But the damage to his brain, nerves, liver, and reflexes is very clear, and so are his spurting fears about nearly everything.

A sleeping-pill suicide, he fell dead with a plate in his hand while just starting a midnight snack. His art, aside from a few last swan notes ("The Forest Path to the Spring" in *Hear Us O Lord from Heaven Thy Dwelling Place*), had died ten years earlier. This was a good man! a tremendous innocent, loved by his friends. A genius—when dry. But after early success he hardly allowed the fog to lift long enough to get his true bearings on his confused novel series *The Voyage that Never Ends*. Recovery was possible. But he *liked* to drink, and standing drunk at a bar was his great joy, an exhilaration of chat and projects.

And so he left thousands of pages, ten years' work, ruined by blurry poetizing. Dead in midlife, still in his forties. Still at the bar, waiting for his ship to come in through the window. A wondrous man who tried to lock in the glow of his talent with a chemical, believing his drunken, non-writing moments would feed light into his work. And in the end, sleeping pills for that mind that beheld such wonder of water and trees and mountains and tides and snow and deer. Every glittering image and beast that moved in the light of his mind, put out.

Closer to home, on the Lower East Side, Jack Kerouac became what Allen Ginsberg calls "the last of the great Christian drinkers," an epithet I'd call horseshit. You don't say the last of the great Christian epileptics, do you? This mysticalizing is the kind of high manure that kept Kerouac an active drunk. It's pouring romance over the corpse.

Kerouac's biographer Ann Charters says he wrote *every-thing* on booze or pot or benny or morphine, and that one sweetwinepiece had him thinking he was Shakespeare/Joyce. His deepest problem was a vast lack of self-esteem he masked with sometimes monstrous grandiosity, thinking himself the greatest stylist since Wolfe and Joyce and Proust and the artistic equal of Shakespeare—which shows the narcissistic grip of the booze-prose octopus. In John Clellon Holmes's elegy to Kerouac "Gone in October," Ginsberg explains that Jack was writing about the Creation emerging from the Void, the perfect emptiness of origins, "the agony of differentiated consciousness. He knew it was all a dream." Holmes himself asks "Why did he drink like that?" and answers that "drink temporarily seemed to stabilize his psychic ground," and because he had no "saving cynicism" and was "insatiably gregarious" when drinking but otherwise not easily sociable, and because he was preoccupied "by the enigma of his own identity." He thought he had noble origins, and he liked saloons "because he had no other place to go," since "the fraternal warmth for which his whole soul longed" had been exiled "to the outer edges of life in the America of his time." And indeed, in Jack's writing, the whole middle range of life is largely ignored, and all's edged with paranoia and exhaustion.

In his *Diary of a Writer* Dostoievsky says about a drunkard, "In his own explanation as to why he took to drinking, there is something false, something unexplained and strained, whereas the matter could have been presented much more simply and clearly." And our dead writer himself, speaking far more openly about his drinking than his friends have managed, said simply and clearly, "How glum life is without the booze." He drank because he was an alcoholic. This insidious disease tells you you don't have it. He had it and knew it.

But he had to defend his illness to go on booze-writing, and he defended it with insane boorishness, despite suicidal remorse. He drank because he wanted to drink more than not drink. And all the con jobs—art, poverty, environment, heredity, despair, sex, death, loneliness, existential angst about the horrors of the age—remain con jobs. So he plucked down the biggest guilt-killer he could find and wrapped himself in Eastern sayings and wore a Golden Eternity Mask, and behind it all sat the real man, feeling timid and worthless. He died at forty-seven. And for the last few years, each morning, he'd have a scotch and gently start the snowball rolling downhill for another day, until night would come and he'd light a candle on the kitchen table, and his midnight energies would arise, the prose coasting and blazing like a Mississippi paddlewheeler down a summer night. Endless pages, ripe and gorgeous, a dreamsweep of redgold paragraphs, the alcohol surging and poetizing about alcohol while he and his memories were just a taxi for the sensations to burn in. I half-think of alcohol not as inert ethyl but rather as an active killer-pest. With Jack Kerouac there was always payment exacted: sufferings, guilt, tears, heaving into his face in the toilet bowl, the bile and cockbeating, and then striving again for the moonlight mood and a few burning phrases. All this self-imposed forsakenness, and his work forever falling short of the medals he awarded himself. The cure? some straight scotch, a beer, or a little bourbon in the breakfast coffee, that's all he'd need, the snowball rolling still again, spending the day building up feelings, cravings for the past, smiles of homey triumph as he wanders about his paid for house mixing with homefeelings for the gutter, for bars and greased elbows and trouble with his cigarette, that whole numb vacation from himself with cronies and the utter boredom of their tales, and at last the weirdly intense nostalgia of evening twilight as he headed for his writingtable and a few charged, wonderful hours at the task of Shakespeare . . . burning words . . . though, unlike Jack, Shakespeare was forever looking outside himself for writing matter, once he got past the sublime whine of his sonnets.

Jack's 211th jazz chorus from *Mexico City Blues* is tagged by Holmes and Charters as his finest statement about why he was killing himself. It begins:

The wheel of the quivering meat conception
Turns in the void expelling human beings

and ends

Poor! I wish I was free of the slaving meat wheel and safe in
heaven dead.

This hangover special was written at thirty-two, with fifteen
years to go before he was safe in heaven dead. To key his adult
life and drinking career to this poem is to suggest that he
stopped growing at the sonnet-writing stage. Maybe in Mexico
he wasn't thinking of a meat wheel but rather feeling his special
Chinese water torture, the continuous soft punch of alcohol
breaking his spirit, rummying his mind, boring holes through
his stomach. And to get his mind off this fierce habit he drove
his typewriter the way his hero Neal Cassady hit the road.
When Jack wrote *On the Road* he could still make energy from
alcohol; he was young, his liver not cooked. He wrote the first
draft in three weeks on benny, his legs swelling with phlebitis.
He rewrote this draft for awhile, then found sketching, or
spontaneous prose, and wrote *Visions of Cody* in his new
sketch style as an in-depth *On the Road*. Off and on he spent
eight years revising *Road* through several more drafts and,
with Malcolm Cowley's suggested editorial cuts, brought forth
what we now have. Which is not a benny-pot-booze glare but a
carefully shaved story—funny, moving, focused. *Visions of
Cody* is a mess that begins enticingly, fades, and picks up after
page 275. It's the least revised of all his big books and has the
largest ballast of sheer bilge—and a few intense passages he
never surpassed. He liked it the best of all his books, just as
Faulkner thought one of his feeblest novels, *A Fable*, was his
masterpiece. Brain burnished, Jack Burnwords hangs with hair
falling over his kitchen pages, hearing the phrases in his
candleflame—he actually wrote by a candle! In the morning a
slug to lock him back into his moonlight mood as he rereads last
night's dreamsong. Despite promises, get that haze fast before

the noon sun hurts your ego, Jack. By God, you've done it again, not perfect but the ol' energy's really there, that prose is coasting. But that last one's not staying down. He hangs over the white toilet bowl and eyes his blood. Ahh, more suffering to spread like butter down the next beat page of forsakenness. Jack London did it the fast way, on a morphine overdose. Mal Lowry got his Golden Eternity Mask on fifty sodium amytals after his wife smashed his gin bottle—he really showed her. Hart Crane jumped unknowingly into a shark's mouth in the Caribbean, surely he'd meant only to drown himself not get eaten alive. Lucky James Agee just felt his heart go and one sunny day Scott Fitzgerald just keeled over, knocking his head on the mantle. Kerouac liked to foster an early dust-jacket bio of himself as a skid-row slob while in truth he was always getting home to mama's spotless house every night or phoning her for money whenever broke. Skid-row barrooms—sure, that's where he could watch the *bad* drunks, the guys who can't hold it, watch them slide into the meat-void. Nothing metaphysical, it's daily suicide cell by cell when your books don't match your self-awarded medals, but you go on over the kitchen table in soupdrenched boredom finishing the last thousand pages of your legend and cooking yourself half-wetbrained as you grind on, jaw slack on chemicals. And in the morning you palm a beer behind mama's back. Jack was self-exiled, and sat by choice down in Florida. To say, with Holmes, that he was "exiled to the outer edges of life in the America of his times" is dumfounding nonsense. Booze is not an artistic or occupational problem: there are as many drunken sanitation workers, brain surgeons, priests and car thieves as there are drunken writers, painters, actors and ad men. And musicians. You might as well say about a Bronx housewife on the sauce that the warmth she longs for has been exiled to the outer edges of life in the America of her time, it's that empty an alibi. Alcohol sucked Jack into such swollen selfconcern, unfeelingness for others, and easy anger, that his only strength was in the lift of tears, righteous indignation, disappointment, lies, heavy sadness, excuses, pride, swift self-lashings, grandiosity, sentimentality, vague spiritual yearnings, breastbeating, boozy homefeelings, and a nice drunk with bolstering fellow boozers. What's the quick cure for so much failure per nerve, when the critics jump on your booze prose, and the world's shams and mockery are just too gloomy?—why, *just one more,* a farewell sip of golden candleglow as you crawl off to the big crib with the dancing bears. That's offensive? Why didn't some friend tell him, Playtime's over, Jack, get honest with yourself, this is the feeblest book you've ever written. Perhaps they had their own self-indulgent writing to defend. But it was possible for Jack to admit powerlessness over the bottle and arrive at a manageable life, free from booze glooms and madness, jitters, trots, deetees, and his morning prayer in the shitbowl. If he could have shelved his ego along with his alibis . . . That the greatest writing is made out of loneliness and despair magnified by booze is an idea for arrested adolescents. Twenty thousand in the bank, downing two fifths of scotch daily, and gone to his golden eternity with a ruptured stomach bleeding massively. Genius is no excuse for self-destruction.

If you read Anne Sexton you'll think lady drunks have special problems of moods and ego, and a painful sensitivity and suffering only they can know. I don't think alcohol really cares. In his memoir of Edna St. Millay, *The Indigo Bunting,* Vincent Sheean describes her last days: "Miss Millay was, to put it bluntly, a frightening apparition to many of us. Her temperament was so variable that it was impossible to tell what mood might overwhelm her next; and she was so painfully sensitive that any untoward phrase or sudden noise could thrust her into a private hell from which she might not emerge for days. She had been going through a bad time . . . a suffering human being whose dolor could be felt like electricity across a room . . . she was terrified. Her terror communicated itself and created terror. I hardly dared to look at her . . ." (pp. 35-36). She was found dead in the dark at the bottom of stairs, a little wineglass beside her. She was on her way for a refill.

Alcoholism is a great leveler of the sexes, it's the same walking death: I can't handle it, pour me another. And it's bad news to get well!—the vocabulary of recovering isn't colorful. What's left to write about? But there really are sober women who let life in rather than stomp it, who have subliminal gifts denied to male eyes, and who speak frankly about the hard facts of pain and blood but also about the full life of the sensibilities, not just about broken glass, knives, bedlam, fungus, wet shadows, loss and ravaged femininity, but also about the ties of family, the practice of hope. Let me speak up for real life, briefly. It isn't always Macbeth's dagger, the handle toward your hand. John Bunyan, no drinker but a writer and father, had to spend ten years in jail. Midway, he tells us in his memoir *Grace Abounding*, he was released on the condition that he wouldn't preach; but speak he did and the authorities threw him back in to serve five more years. He writes:

> The parting with my wife and my poor children hath often been to me as the pulling of my flesh from my bones, especially my poor blind child who lay nearer my heart than all I had besides. Poor child, thought I, what sorrow art thou like to have for thy portion in this world. Thou must be beaten, must beg, suffer hunger, cold, nakedness, and a thousand calamities, though I cannot now endure that the wind should blow upon thee. But yet I must venture you all with God, though it goeth to the quick to leave you.

Here is real life at its most agonized, but Bunyan writes it straight out, flat, and yet with a power that defies breastbeating and gloom-mongering. It is possible to write from strength about the worst calamities in your life. You don't have to suck your thumb every time you stub your little toe. But enough uplift.

In a letter to his wife's psychiatrist, our gentleman novelist Scott Fitzgerald writes that he didn't start drinking to boost his working spirit until he was thirty. Until then, he says, he

wrote on cup after cup of coffee, at last to rise white and
trembling from his desk to face his sick wife over the dinner
table while the first aperitif was served. This drink made her
even more unstable but wine was a necessity for him in
withstanding her long monologues about her dance obsession
and her glazed eye toward any other subject. But, he told her
doctor, he'd be a pig not to experiment with stopping drinking
entirely for six months. And see what happens. Maybe even
continue the experiment thereafter, if successful! But to
forswear wine forever, no. Wine is an amenity, when the world
is at its brightest. He admits he's abused liquor and must pay
for it with suffering "and death perhaps but not with renuncia-
tion." Wine at day's end is one of the rights of man! Any human
value he might have would disappear if he condemned himself
to a lifelong asceticism to which he is not adapted either by
habit, temperament or the circumstances of his metier.

A cry for the good life, it carries weight—or it did for him.
There was little real knowledge of the workings of the alcoholic
mind in the early thirties when he wrote this letter. And as any
alcoholic will, he's looking for a sanction to continue controlled
drinking. The controlled drinker who is an active alcoholic is
even worse off and living under a greater strain than the
drinker who just says oh hell and drinks himself every which
way drunk. His controlled drinking meant concern with small
amounts, which bound him in pianowire restraints, self-
torture, miserly measurements, and the morning count on the
bed's edge: Did I have three ounces or four last night? If I skip
today, I can have double tomorrow at the party, no the party is
Friday so if I skip tomorrow too then I can have triple at the
party—and really get smashed. And so on into infinite divisions
and ounce-splittings, until his whole day is quietly, insanely
tuned into the song in the drops saved here, added there.

He later saw through his own arrogance (his word) and
gullibility, but not until passing through several hospitalizations and a staggering history of self-made disasters. And not
before compromising his last completed masterpiece, a novel

conceived in a superrich Keatsian deathglow of mothwing textures and melancholy elaborations. Years later he complained to his editor that this novel's artistic and commercial failure rested on his having finished the last third on alcohol. He revised it, but died before the republication. The sober version is clear and strong, but most bookfolk prefer the first and foggy version. It's more smiling-through-Keats. His last year of life was spent abstinent and in a state of profound regeneration—he was *not* hopeless! For his last and soberest novel he tossed out Keats and his own famous ornamental prose, and there rose up in him a strikingly naked intelligence peering hard at real people stripped of their fevery fogs and glamour. His wife twitted that she could smell the heroine's underarm shields. These unfinished pages are a testament to his private and sacred trust with himself. His inspiration was no longer chemical. These pages also echo the comment of his great drinking buddy Ring Lardner, a fellow writer who died in his forties (as did he), who said, "No one, ever, wrote anything as well after even one drink as he would have done without it."

The Boston author and bestselling prizewinner John Marquand would fire his secretary if he or she did not join him for noon martinis after his morning stint and in preparation for afternoon rewriting. His pages have the even flow of a wall-to-wall martini, no rise, no fall, just flat gray. His second wife died dead drunk in the bathroom, having slipped and fallen headfirst into a full bathtub, where she drowned—a case of life outwriting the polished hack she'd divorced. He kept his glow on but one rarely saw Marquand drunk. He spaced his ounces, lived to enjoy his wealth and comforts—the image of what I started out to be at nineteen when first sitting in my garage typing a mystery. Before switching to big fiction, he wrote one hundred and ten serials for *The Saturday Evening Post*, all forgotten, unless you remember Peter Lorre as Mr. Moto. Edmund Wilson, reviewing *Repent in Haste*, said "a novel by J. P. Marquand is simply a neat pile of typewritten manuscript." He was that rarity, a heavy drinker who stopped short at womanizing and an ulcer and remained on the near side of alcoholism. He's here as a benchmark.

Falling over the bench is my favorite mystery stylist Raymond Chandler who, at sixty-four, tried to kill himself in his bathroom. He decided to shoot himself in the shower. The first shot went off without his intending it to, poor drunk. The trigger pull was so light that he barely touched it when off it went, the bullet ricocheting around the tiles and going out through the ceiling. The second shot, which he meant to be the real business, didn't fire at all. The charge had decomposed. Then he blacked out. A cop found him sitting on the floor of the shower trying to get the gun into his mouth. He later said he had absolutely no sense of guilt or embarrassment when meeting townspeople who'd heard on the radio all about his fiasco. Ahead of him lay six years of relapses and hospitalizations, but to the end he was a clear-minded stylist with a dry twist to his diction, and would say in one of his last letters that he had "more love for our superb language than I could ever possibly express." He died on the sauce, with a side order of pneumonia.

Fist-happy John O'Hara broke his own stereotype by not dying on the sauce in his forties. He missed by only a hair. At forty-eight an erupting ulcer and swollen liver nearly killed him, and he stopped by himself and stayed stopped for seventeen years, not just willingly dry but fully sober. He engaged in wide social activity, was a happy man in a sunburst of the big works he'd been denying himself for years. He remarried and was mindful of the graces, some might think overly mindful, with friends everywhere, and earning vast forests of cash—he died with a million in his royalty account, had plenty more in private banks, lived handsomely, shone with tailoring, drove a Rolls, and was loved. Corking up forever can be beautiful! And he had a close friend who was also a recovering alcoholic who visited often and gave advice, or at least encouragement, for John would think longingly now and then about a cold beer on a hot day. He wasn't perfect. He sought prizes, had a passionately large sense of the figure he cut, was painfully sensitive to supposed slights, given to lasting anger and spite, and took unkindly to editing, all of which *might have been* qualities made more bitter and violent by drink and which he would have had to defend when sober—or admit to being a fool when tanked. His drinking career was hectic, vicious, fearful, angry, driven by a mania for parties and escape into bistros. In his flight from an Irish-Catholic background, he was scarred by hangovers of unbelievable spikelike intensity—paralyzing! He had a spinning thirst for punishment and was fired from every single job he ever held. And right now he's watching over my shoulder so that I don't mangle the facts. All right, I confess that the latest novel of his I finished was *A Rage to Live* (1948), written while he still had self-admitted "trouble with the sauce," but I don't doubt that *Ten North Frederick, From the Terrace, Ourselves to Know, The Lockwood Concern* and *The Ewings* might be better. I'll never know, most likely, though I have his complete works and enjoy the chunks I take in (he reads well aloud on car trips). He had enviable drive, and a spinal need to excel that carried right over from life to the very granite of his tombstone, on which is the epitaph he wrote for himself: *Better than anyone else, he told the truth about his time, the first half of the twentieth century. He was a professional. He wrote honestly and well.* It's a good-looking stone, I've seen it, but some pro with an eye for excess trimmed out the phrase "the first half of the twentieth century," a span already clearly stated in the two dates under John's name. In many early stories he used a semi-autobiographical newsman, James Malloy, who is plagued by low self-worth, painful feelings of inferiority, and rises eyeball to eyeball clenching his fists after the first ounce. For my money, it was Malloy, still lingering, who carefully spelled out O'Hara's last boast, in granite.

Jack London's *John Barleycorn*, or *Alcoholic Memoirs*, is the story of London's drinking, his early distaste for alcohol, bonding with old salts when he was a young sailor in the

Oakland bars, early days as a writer, and slow addiction after success. He shows himself as not physically given to drink, much more to candy. One-day bouts and binges while growing up were all—except for the time he fell overboard while drunk and tried to swim out with the tide and drown; four hours in the bay sobered him and he saved himself. At first he never used drink to write, was rigid about typing a thousand words daily, no holidays. But when success overcame him (and its taste of ashes), so did the pre-dinner cocktail, the pre-lunch cocktail, then two, then looking forward to lunch and dinner with growing fierceness, taking two drinks to a guest's one, stealing drinks, and lastly drinking alone. Striding through this is Jack London the mighty savage with a head for Nietzsche and Marx, above the urges of booze, and its master, until:

> . . . After a boisterous afternoon in the swimming pool, followed by a glorious ride on horseback over the mountains or up or down the Valley of the Moon, I found myself so keyed and splendid that I desired to be more highly keyed and splendid. I knew the way . . . I was perpetually finding excuses for extra cocktails. It might be the assembling of a particularly jolly crowd; a touch of anger against my architect or against a thieving stonemason working on my barn; the death of my favorite horse in a barbed wire fence; or news of good fortune in the morning mail from my dealings with editors and publishers. It was immaterial what the excuse might be, once the desire had germinated in me. The thing was: I *wanted* alcohol. At last, under a score and more of years of dallying and not wanting, now I wanted it. And my strength was my weakness. I required two, three, or four drinks to get an effect commensurate with the effect the average man got out of one drink.

Despite every sort of happiness, he finds himself ordering doubles regularly.

> One result of this regular heavy drinking was to jade me. My mind grew so accustomed to spring and liven by artificial means that without artificial means it refused to spring and liven.

Alcohol became more and more imperative in order to meet people, in order to become sociably fit. I had to get the kick and the hit of the stuff, the crawl of the maggots, the genial brain glow, the laughter tickle, the touch of devilishness and sting, the smile over the face of things, ere I could join my fellows and make one with them.

But his old sickness, the temptation to suicide, comes back forcefully, and so he begins drinking "rationally, intelligently." A few years' trip on his yacht about the South Seas helps balance periods of sobriety and drunkenness, then it's back to his California ranch, the Valley of the Moon, and drinking "as a broad-shouldered chesty man may drink." He's drinking late at night while reading, waking early hungover, having a pre-breakfast pick-me-up. Wherever he goes visiting he totes two quarts or more in his grip, and achieves "a condition in which my body was never free from alcohol"—

I was carrying a beautiful alcoholic conflagration around with me. The thing fed on its own heat and flamed the fiercer. There was no time, in all my waking time, that I didn't want a drink. I began to anticipate the completion of my daily thousand words by taking a drink when only five hundred words were written. It was not long until I prefaced the beginning of the thousand words with a drink.

You've made it, Jack!

The gravity of this I realized too well. I made new rules. Resolutely I would refrain from drinking until my work was done. But a new and most diabolical complication arose. The work refused to be done without drinking. It just couldn't be one. I had to drink in order to do it. I was beginning to fight now. I had the craving at last, and it was mastering me. I would sit at my desk and daily with pad and pen, but words refused to flow. My brain could not think the proper thoughts because continually it was obsessed with the one thought that across the room in the liquor cabinet stood John Barleycorn. When, in despair, I took my drink, at once my brain loosened up and began to roll off the thousand words . . . Merciful goodness!—if John Barleycorn could get such sway over me, a non-alcoholic, what must be the sufferings of the true alcoholic, battling against the organic demands of his chemistry while those closest to him sympathize little, understand less, and despise and deride him!

And again he's gripped by the "white logic" of suicide: life is a cheat, the mind a fog, the passions full of lies. The Pit waits for all, no matter your life-illusions. Alcohol brings "cosmic sadness" and is the "messenger of truth beyond truth, the antithesis of life, cruel and bleak as interstellar space, pulseless and frozen as absolute zero . . ."

Chapters 36 and 37 of *John Barleycorn*, showing alcoholic hopelessness at its most life-darkening, must be the most powerful pages London ever wrote, and are too long to quote. What they mean to me is that the "white logic" can't be argued against with any hope of yea-saying if you are drinking: the uttermost bleakness and horror of life are beyond an answer from booze. You are playing in alcohol's corner no matter what arguments you come up with. Jack's last thoughts are clear enough:

> . . . my need was mental and social. When I thought of alcohol, the connotation was fellowship. When I thought of fellowship, the connotation was alcohol. Fellowship and alcohol were Siamese twins. They always occurred linked together.

To the end, he did not know he was a drunk! and thought himself a social drinker. He would master alcohol, drink with controls. He lived three more years in the Valley of the Moon, his favorite dinner being two nearly raw wild ducks boiled no more than eight minutes (his wife would gag at the sight), and then Superman came down with nephritis and uremia, his body in a long decay, and he apparently overdosed on two conflicting drugs, morphine and atropine. Suicide?—it was denied by many. And so at forty, the nation's greatest public specimen of ruggedness, denying his hopeless physical breakdown to the last, rationing himself to one cocktail a night and still dreaming he could hold his liquor, died. I never felt closer to him, not in *The Sea Wolf* beloved of my youth, nor my other boyhood favorites of his, than in his horror-pages on the "white logic" and dehumanization of life, in which I experience with him what he truly sought throughout his drinking career—fellowship—as if he were my Siamese twin who didn't make it. We are all supermen, for a while.

Eugene O'Neill, our greatest playwright, became unwillingly dry at thirty-eight. He stopped by himself, on his doctor's advice. He didn't enjoy his recovery. He went right on hugging his theme of "hopeless hope" and became matchless at tragedy, a master of ironic comedy, and emerged from blurry apprenticeship to write four of the finest plays ever staged. His best pages are the highwatermark of American playwrighting. He had unrivaled spiritual intensity in writing about alcohol. To me, and to some of my friends who are also recovering, his alcohol horror stories are rather tame and tearful, but he enriches them magnificently. You can't watch a play from his greatest period without knowing exactly where the bottle is, it is the silver pivot of the action, and makes everyone highflown, fantastic and grim. All the males get viciously silvertongued. They're always ready with a verse of Dowson or Baudelaire or Nietzsche, and can be equally eloquent about their youth or the electric light bill. They love to explode pipe-dreams, but also to describe their most cherished moments. They are all gifted rhetoricians in spiritual communion with language which has been unloosed by the sacred bottle, whose ounces are dispensed like precious tears of God's blood. To drink is family fellowship, a sip of lightning from holy Ireland itself where reverence for alcohol is genetic. They are not florid, they are gab-possessed, every turn of their smart talk has its edge of rage. One hero at last kicks the bottle and is reborn, marvelously coming to his senses, like Don Quixote after a life's madness, but finds his family begging him to go back on the bottle and become his raging old self again. In a later play his hero tries to sober up a whole saloon on the Bowery, but his effort ends in a fizzle, with everybody's pipe-dreams and brain fog rolling back in and all the drunks once more jigging and singing in hopeless hope—ghastly hilarity! His hero had got sober by killing his forgiving and forgiving, saintly, pitying wife whose endless forgiveness enabled him to go right on drinking—until he hated her enough to kill her for her forgiveness. The play's wonderful irony is that while bearing the greatest human sin, murder, the hero can bring his dream-breaking message of freedom from illusion. But his message fails to break the drinkers' bondage to alcohol, since he is only sending them from one illusion to another; each man remains alone and seeks his safety apart: they are not a fellowship, with each bolstering the other. The play's message hits home with me. My view may not be exactly what the playwright meant, but it's what the play says to me: *You can't do it alone.*

Well, you may say, *he* did it alone! Indeed he did, and a hard time he had of it in 1926 when he stopped and when there was no understanding of alcoholism—and there were no fellowships of recovering drinkers. No steady, life-giving spirits to replace "hopeless hope." As for the drunks in that Bowery saloon, the date of the action is 1912, and they could as well have the plague or malaria for all the chance in hell they have to recover. Theirs was an illness the hand of God rarely lifted.

My most moving passage in O'Neill is the twenty-minute moonlight and alcohol monologue by Jamie Tyrone in *A Moon for the Misbegotten*—sheer poetry—despite the fact that I have to smile at Jamie's blaming his habit on a crosscountry trainride with his mother's corpse in the baggage car while he was screwing a hooker day in and out. Sounds great on stage in the myth-enforcing moonlight, and playgoers like it as an "explanation" of his habit, but for me it's only one more self-delusion in Jamie's alibi bag. Jamie drinks because his cells are punchdrunk with thirst and because he feels hopeless about not drinking. It's the tissuing butchery of his self-analysis while souped up by drink that moves me. I was just such a Chinese juicehead myself, looking for the first cause which, when pricked, would release me from my disease. Christ, it's beautiful, pipesmoke in the moonlight, all that analysis and heartbreak. The audience hears the big explanation which Jamie is later too hungover to recall. It makes you feel five hundred thousand pounds lighter, like dying in your sleep— but it's a phony.

It's spooky being an active drunk, waking up dead. Your body ashes, eyelids glued tight, brain shut down. Day after day climbing out of the grave, once more to fight the jimjams, the whammies, the quivers and quavers, the juice show, the spooks. Outfoxing anxieties was hard work, took skill, craft, deep reserves, an ability to rise again and again from our little suicides. We brought a narcissistic care to our drinking, devised rites against bad spirits and jujus. Ernest Hemingway loved to go into the Gulf Stream and fish for the big ones. He had a sharp eye for spooks and rites to ward them off. He could gauge cold-loss by the sweat on his cork-lined gin tonics, and measure the thermodynamics of icecube-melt balanced against sun-heat, time of day, wind, drinking rate per glass, ounces per day, and relate all this to his body weight, work schedule, fishing schedule, recovery schedule. Never was a writer more worried about spirits, wine and gin spirits, animal spirits, personal, human and otherwise, writing spirits, spirits of places to write in, or to go back to and heal in. He has a furtive, beset look in later pictures, a pained grin, as anguished and tragic as Teddy Roosevelt's—both were lionhunters (*wham!* shoot those spooks) and both lost their reason, the great will they shared crumbling before shapeless fears and threats of doom. Had he taken alcohol out of his life, he might have held his craziness within manageable limits. Who can say? Crazy folks shouldn't drink, it's like throwing gasoline onto a banked fire. His repeated suicide tries, hospitalizations, shock treatments, longtime sleeplessness, high blood pressure and tension, severe hepatitis, jaundice, enlarged liver, dark piss, swollen ankles, cold fury about his self-woundings, broken toes and bones, head wounds, accidents, fist fights, black eyes, and relentless spiritual maiming, his tears when the work just wouldn't come anymore, his unbearable boasting and trembling openness to danger (he thought)—all should have warned him about his lifelong heavy drinking. Instead, he drank to the bitter finish, and sank into unbudgeable mawkishness that led to blowing his brains out, or self-pity carried beyond repair. When you're really crazy, one drink will spark it, shoot up tears like Vesuvius.

For my money, his books go straight downhill after *A Farewell to Arms* and *Winner Take Nothing*, aside from the magnificent reprieve of *The Old Man and the Sea* and most of *A Moveable Feast*. *For Whom the Bell Tolls* is his worst great book. I love its haunting effects and nature-writing but when the characters speak I fear I hear horseshit plopping. What's more, I read Robert Jordan's big monologue about democracy and fascism as a battle between the right to drink and the temperance bogeys, and easily the most strained and unconvincing pages he ever published. Our spooks take on elaborate disguises. A writer friend of mine tells of Papa going into the Floridita bar in Havana and asking a crony what he was drinking. Nothing, the crony said, he'd just joined Alcoholics Anonymous. Hemingway paled, moved to the farthest point of the bar and stood muttering to himself. He was a defensive and bare-nerved perfectionist when any hint of criticism arose about his drinking. There are long lab analyses of his physical breakdown, which witness his spellbinding martyrdom to death by the ounce. By his forties he'd gone out one ounce too far and the youthful metabolism he later hymned in his memoirs was lost, and the power of juice to give life, energy and spirit would never return. At the last it gave only a brief vacation from ego-ridden powerlessness and being absolutely spooked. My heart goes out to that shadowboxer and his last fourteen years of suffering with the alcoholic perfectionist who finally out-feinted him. And laid him out.

Manic acts of inappropriate behavior surround Theodore Roethke, the huge, mystical nature poet whose legend shows him standing on his classroom desk and tommy-gunning his students. His adult life boiled with mad acts. He knew better than anyone else how crazy he was, drinking for him like toedancing across the frame of a greenhouse—he could get badly cut or killed. He died on mint juleps, while swimming, his heartwalls sticking together. He was often hospitalized, and once given shock treatments. You'd think he'd know better than to drink, but this cunning disease offers feelings of instant success and riotous fame to one who lusts after them as he did—toward the end he was looking for a Nobel. His gorilla antics and tree-swinging exuberance don't explain anything; they only point toward his opposing black gloom and deep sobs and suckings. Many symptoms often heralded a breakdown: he became excited, cheerful, alarmed, eager, his voice flowed without stop, great plans ballooned, he wore three pairs of trousers at once, rubbers on dry days, and an old widebrimmed unblocked Borsalino was a strong signal to friends of his impending derangement. He'd go without sleep, phone dozens of friends all over the country and abroad, and slip into feelings of great wealth and power. He thought he was made of steel and once told some hospital attendants, "You'd better tie me down, give me a mouth gag—I took on five docs at the last place!" This is garden-variety alcoholism, with no need of a clinical label. Who needs a label when, during his stay at one West Coast mental hospital and finding the institutional food unsatisfactory, he'd send out for prime beef and run his bill up with cases of ale? During his last two years he was frequently manic, exhilarated, feeling enormously free and drinking to control his boundless spirit. He always tried to control his manic states. First thing in the morning would be a glass of beer and later in the day whiskey, which he thought he used as a depressant. Alcohol is a depressant, but for crazy folks it's not the best drug.

Another manic gargantuan, Thomas Wolfe got me drunk on life, gave me a larger-than-life appetite for drunkenness and led me into lonesome drinking for the sheer glow of it. To grow into his mask was impossible and I let serve instead the superaware sensibilities I thought alcohol granted. I was an impressionable ninth-grade dropout when I began reading him. Meanwhile *he* had been drinking to become James Joyce, who himself died of a perforated duodenal ulcer, the result of drink, and which had him writhing like a fish in the ambulance to his last hospital. I began reading Wolfe for his art, his next goat-cry or extravagant set-piece, just as I read Joyce to experience what language can do out there at its limits. And I ended by searching through biographies of both these geniuses to find some sanction that would allow me to drink as they did—I took all their manias and ulcers as badges of glory—as I did with all my gods, their broken bones, their arrests, their madhouses, the grief of their wives and children, it all came with the package, and especially narcissistic self-absorption chemically enlarged. All these boozers on their mountaintops wrestling with their genius—what better life can there be?

As for the writer who baptized me, Wolfe was a devoutly honest man, extremely sensitive to wounded feelings in others (being oversensitive himself), but was cursed with morbid suspiciousness. Few could talk to him about his drinking, or would dare, he was six-foot-six, two-hundred-and-fifty pounds, and such a powerful talker, with a disarming, childish directness and yet odd originality of word choice that overwhelmed listeners (he was always polishing stories by mouth before writing them): a million-worded steamroller who knew not the hour of the night.

Tubercular, a heavy smoker, often feverish, he was the son of a life-gulping, roaring alcoholic whose binges often hospitalized him. My baptizer's most famous drinks were at the Munich *Oktoberfest,* in a sea-slop of double-strength beer, a great smoky hell of beer, where a brawl hospitalized him for a week; and an epic week's binge with Nobel winner Sinclair Lewis in London, which Wolfe used as a bravura set-piece in his last novel, there drawing a picture of himself as considerably more sober than was true. When dining at someone's house, his capacity for drink was such that the wise host put a bottle of scotch and pitcher of water by his chair, so he could replenish without interrupting his talk. When his work troubled him and plunged him into the manic-depressive's trough, his drinking swelled and he would hurl himself about his room like a madman. His long-suffering editor Maxwell Perkins knew from bitter experience that a quiet drink with him could be explosive. His suspicion and fear could settle on the most harmless man at a bar and drive him to pick a fight. One evening, when he and Perkins (who was half his weight) were dining at Cherio's, he turned on him in a state of murderous drunkenness and threatened to knock him down and stood swinging his arms to get ready. His editor took him outside for the fight, but he was defused when a strange brunette ran up to his tall bulk and cried, "This is what I came to New York to see!"—he was already very famous. A Southern friend recalls him tossing down a full waterglass of whiskey as if it were mild red wine, then finishing a pint (but for the heel) and walking six miles home, hatless and coatless, in drizzling rain. Another old friend, in 1937, a year before his death, said she couldn't bear to see him burn himself out and "butcher his genius with liquor." When his second novel appeared, he went into a three-day blackout in Paris. In his last year, drinking and brooding for a week, he ran into Sherwood Anderson in a hotel lobby and told the old writer that his later work had let everybody down, completely estranging Anderson. A month short of thirty-eight, he died of brain tuberculosis. His work had become less swamped with emotion, clearer, but hardly stronger, since his strongest vein was the Whitmanlike set-piece which gave his descriptive energies full play, and this vein's force had dimmed greatly. His despair was building, his language changing and less gripping; his strongest, most focused novel might have lain ten years ahead, after World War Two, a subject equal to his full ripening. But his warnings of early death proved true, and he died without having to grapple fully with his ghosts in the bottle or the swelling pressures of alcoholism.

He was my god and, as I've said, his was Joyce who himself had a drinking problem—though Joyce did not think himself a drunk since he did not drink before five in the afternoon, on working days, which *proved* he wasn't a drunk. Even so, *Finnegans Wake* is a great bubble of ruby-red exhalations of spirit, and Joyce himself, in Ellmann's great biography, examples the classic evasions, self-deceits, and symptoms, including his brick-red drinker's face and death by ruptured ulcer. Wolfe once rode on a bus from Brussels to Waterloo with the Joyces, without introducing himself, and later wrote his mistress about it, saying that he liked Joyce's "highly colored, slightly concave" face with its thin mouth, "not delicate but extraordinarily humorous" and its "large powerful straight nose—redder than his face" and "somewhat pitted with scars and boils . . ."

This classic floridity reappears in Sinclair Lewis, the Nobel winner with whom Wolfe binged in London—a week-long drunk for bottle colossi which Wolfe rolls off for over fifty pages in *You Can't Go Home Again* ("Lloyd McHarg"— Lewis—has a face that seems "to be all dried out and blistered by the fiery flames that burned in it"). His alcoholism was such a dancing horror that anything I say is a stop-motion study. Nearly all drunks are nuisances but Lewis was a sodden, frenzied, furniture-smashing nuisance beyond belief, and finally, when crossed, became an insane, jerking skeleton (Schorer's massive *Sinclair Lewis* is second only to Blotner's two-volume *Faulkner* for detail on the active writer-drunk). Barred from the bistro "21" one evening in 1932, he sat on the curb of Fifty-Second Street sighing, "What's the use of winning the Nobel Prize if it doesn't get you into speakeasies?" His life was one of noisy desperation; his talk a tremendous entertainment, filled with wheeling whimsies and mimicry, but at last tiresome, void of conversation, just show, show, show, prove, prove his mercurial brightness, despite bounding senselessness. At thirty-six he thought nothing of emptying a pint of whiskey straight down in one hoist, without chaser, which is neither gracious nor social but frankly insane—and courting death. And he drank in this ruinous fashion for thirty more years, writing five solid satires in the twenties, then entering a soul-flattening decline upon receipt of the Nobel Prize. His drinking was to quench the sense of unutterable ridiculousness and unworthiness forever burning him like a skin disease.

His joker's swirl through endless disaster is grotesque and horrific, the tale of a cackling dead man racing from accident to accident. He was one of the worst writers who ever lived, but wrote a personally stamped sentence, and for ten years he gripped the world with the wondrously clear focus he brought to bear upon life in the States. And then, his habit demanding the income, he hacked out a novel a year and published it, good or bad, lying to himself, loving his worst works and sentimentalizing them. Often leaping in talk from the tender to the slashing, he'd go pokerfaced, look out at you and sneer *"You stinking hypocrite!"* and then forget he'd been talking to you. There is nothing good to say about his drinking; it inspired nothing but a deadend shuffle to oblivion. Hospital upon hospital, his pitted face becoming ugly and red when drunk, raging nerves, raging anger against himself, hallucinations in which he wandered about searching for the stairway of a vanished house, death in acute delirium tremens, his body poisoned to the marrow. No fear on earth could keep him sober, and he had no friends but cronies. He died among strangers, in a strange clinic outside Rome, his hospital record reading meaninglessly "Paralysis of the heart." God spare us all, gentlemen.

But there are so many others. The poets especially seem hard hit with lives of desperate, drunken melancholy, destruction ounce by ounce and then the full weight of suicide. Many suffered unnecessarily from a brilliant fog of treacherously uninspired myopic metaphors. The alcohol works, or misses, perhaps according to the degree of brain damage the poet sustains—those cells really do burn out. And don't grow back.

You can still write damned well without all your brain cells alive, but the emotional and spiritual damage to your wind calls forth nervous shortcuts across the plain sense of your work, or demands surreal, private seven-league leaps of imagination only the poet himself can later follow, with luck. This is personal, of course, and subjective. But the deetees, hospitalizations, suicides, the autopsy reporting "Insult to the brain" (as with Dylan Thomas)—these madnesses speak for themselves about the capacity for simple plain sense and the breakdown in poetic imagery.

The suicides come in clutches. Others die of heart attacks, pneumonia, cirrhosis, kidney failure, ulcers, those are the main ways to die from alcoholism if you've given up driving. Few writers die directly of alcohol, say with a massive stomach rupture; they die of organic breakdown. And coroners cover it up for the family, no family wants an accredited alcoholic, not even a literary family. There's not much you can say when she shoves her head into the stove, or he locks himself into the garage with the car running. But otherwise, if it's physical, put down *stroke* or *heart failure*. The poet falls dead in his hotel hallway or convulses in a taxicab and it's called natural causes. If it's a dark night on the highway and he throws himself in front of a car . . . well, maybe he just staggered. But if John Berryman jumps off a high bridge onto an ice-covered river, we admit suicidal depression and skim over alcoholism, particularly since this poet hadn't had a drink for a year.

This suicide died dry.* He wrote a memoir (*Recovery*) describing his dry year, and it's a potent guide on how not to recover. First you hang onto all your old romances about your illness, then you suck your old grandiosity for every drop that's still in it, you resist deflation at depth of the alcoholic ego, you vigorously emphasize your uniqueness among those clods who

---

*Dry: not drinking but sour, dispirited, keeping apart (Lone Wolf), bottlefighting, angry, boring to self and others, self-pitying, big baby (I want, I want), hanging onto symptoms, resisting getting well, still full of alcoholic attitudes, insane, and spiritually inert.

Sober: striving toward wholeness and serenity through fellowship.

might be recovering with you, and then you defend to the death your right to self-destruction. Well, this man was scarred from boyhood by his father's shooting himself just outside the boy's bedroom window. He seems to have spent his life distracting himself from a repeat act, by himself, and so he wrote and rushed like a frantic waterspider over a surge of puns, wisecracks, blackface imitations, surface brilliancies, scholarly prolixities, leaps in tense, voice, time, hoohaws, whispers, solemn throbs of tearful spiritual praise, and hid behind many masks per line. His greatest resource was Old Giantkiller hundred proof, aside from womanizing, but he could not lay his dad's phantom. His favorite drinking epithet was that he felt "hot as a pistol." Dad's? Don't get me wrong—I don't think he suicided from some Freudian abscess about his father. After long exposure to the soft punch of alcohol, drop, drop, drop, drop, drop, the original reason for drinking gives way to the craving: you drink because you want it and need it, drink because you drink. No alibi is needed, either medical, artistic or religious: the illness is ego, with its exaggerated pride and balancing lack of self-esteem, its intolerance, hatred of change and resistance to getting well, grandiose talk and behavior—"You simply do not understand that I drink because it is expected of me as a poet who celebrates the Divine Mysteries of Life, for Christ's sake. Do you realize that *I* am in line for a Nobel? That it was strongly suggested by *Life* Magazine and by Spacefiller of the *Times* that my name should certainly be put in contention? If these *facts* mean anything at all to you, you just might *shut up.*"—diseased, alcoholic ego. Recovery isn't based on uncovering that mystical *first cause* (divine repetition). You dig up something about your childhood, or you come to terms with some grief in your past, or you finally get over the hump of your sexual despair and maybe marry—that's not going to take away the first drink. It'll always be out there . . . waiting for you. You're never recovered. Ever. Nor was he.

Nor did he die for poetry. Nobody dies for poetry or art.

You *live* for poetry. You suicide out of misguided self-pity. He feared the complete humiliation of the alcoholic ego which precedes the first life of the healthy ego. He wouldn't give it up: it would compromise the confusion he'd tried to ennoble as poetry while an active drunk. Starting fresh meant that a massive part of his work so far was self-pity and breastbeating. This was the last mask he couldn't rip off, it was like tearing the beard from his cheeks. Too, too painful. Too much invested. He was pitted against his contemporaries, who were his stock-in-trade as a witty, liverish, bitter commentator, fee-paid. For him, loneliness was life, fellowship death, death the last refuge of the alcoholic ego. The suicide refuses to yield up his sickness. Berryman's was a font of self-torture as he tried to ease into a high spiritual tone in his last poems, *Delusions, Etc.*, and then stabbed each poem as it was written, discarding it with "white logic" for the next, tightening the little steel circle of nitpicking which would keep him sick forever. Alone at the core of hysteria, he marries his thumb.

Despite demeaning failures, limbo hospitalizations, tries for recovery and repeated relapses, these writers toweringly resist and consistently fail to recognize home truths about themselves. Despite the merciless twistings and turnings of their craving. False allegiances abound: to culture and place of birth, to so-called social graces, to male bonding in war or sports or hunting, to "literature" and the fellowship of dead drunks, and to living companions at their manly self-sacrifice to Old Ego-giant. Not to forget an allegiance to the nobility of bourbon itself.

Our Southern writers are not doing well. William Faulkner, our greatest Southerner, had a writing peak that lasted for about eight years, during his thirties. Something disastrous happened when he turned forty; whatever grip he had on his alcoholism faded, and so did the hot focus of his imagination. He wrote for twenty-two more years, but his brain was stunned—not that you could tell it by looking at him. What we get from his later decades is the famous mannered diction, senatorial tone, a hallucinated rhetoric of alcohol full of ravishing musings and empty glory. Dead junk beside the cloudburst pages of his thirties. Once he surrendered to his manner, he could no longer recover his ecstasy of words springing from his heart rather than his head. All his living breath-rhythms became shaped and labored marble phrases, each sentence absolute as stone.

His life became hospitals. He was too proud to drop his masks, his riding bowler and granite mustache, that pose as master of Latinate diction, his alcoholic hardening of the ego. He spoke of "enduring" and "anguishing" and "prevailing" and all this meant was that he would suffer his disease impassively. He expounded resistance to recovery as if it were *the* necessary human condition. It became the Southern heritage, the alcoholic stoic standing under his front portico while the noble agrarians crumbled under greed, incest, murder and the horrors of the night. That there might be some help for all this was not part of his pitiless universe. For me, this unlifting grey gloom is just as relentlessly sentimental a picture of life as anything in Pollyanna or the worlds of Disney or soap opera or the sorrows in romance fiction.

Whenever he visited Manhattan, his publishers and editors had their hands full; this sacred monster required chaperoning, often was hospitalized. He told one editor that his first drinks had been given him by his grandfather, he always got the last drops in the old man's glass. But later he drank, he said, to ease the pain that lingered from his airplane crackup. But mostly, *mostly*, his drinking was "a matter of chemistry." He could manage weeks or months of drinking at a normal gait, which for him was two bourbons at lunch, two more at five, a martini before dinner, a half bottle of wine with it, and perhaps two more bourbons to nurse during the evening. Then, out of the blue, the craving would come. He'd fight it off. Then something would happen that would "get me all of a turmoil inside"—and the only escape was liquor. Then a situation would arise that he couldn't cope with, and he'd crumble under the chemistry of craving. And then he was off and running, bingeing toward limbo, the crackup, the hospital.

This rationale of "the chemistry of craving" evades everything really wrong with his habits: it was the daily punch, punch, punch of just two bourbons at lunch (he was a clockwatcher avid for noon), just two more after five, just a martini before dinner, and just half a bottle of wine, and just another bourbon or two (how many ounces when *you* poured them?) to nurse during the evening that kept his disease active and simmering, why not say flaring. All drunks lie about quantities, forget the hidden nips in the kitchen, cellar, barn, the very dry double martini they call a single, the farewell nightcap to another lush day of "controlled" drinking. Then he affects amazement and turmoil about this strange craving that horripilates our backs and arms and dries the tongue until we're "corroded as a Spad on a movie lot," as the poet Jack McManis puts it, and sitting ducks for just one more. Talk about "anguishing." All this talk about the tide of doom, the drinking heritage from his grandfather, the mystery of chemistry, and his dreadful fight to control his sipping is a feeble defense against the clear need for total abstinence, and an attempt to build an intellectual dam against a Mississippi of self-pity and chemical overcast. But alcoholism is not an intellectual problem (his wife Estelle joined A.A.). Faulkner's Manhattan editor, Robert Linscott, said of him: "You would be aware of the symptoms of increasing tension—drumming fingers, evasive looks, monosyllabic replies to questions—then he'd disappear, and, when you next heard of him, he'd be out cold." Numberless hospitalizations for alcoholic exhaustion, deetees, whiskey ulcers, electroshock therapy, the endless bloody nicks and gashes on his head, broken ribs, falls down stairs, falls from horses, plane crackups, broken vertebrae, sweats, shakes, organic damage, fibrillation, blackouts, in Egypt, France, Greece, Virginia, Memphis, Manhattan, waking in the booze wards of the world. Not an intellectual problem.

There's so much I must leave out! I'm barely into all the dead drunks just of American writing, the grapes of Steinbeck, the poets, more ladies, the humorists—James Thurber sits here turning red. "I qualify, I qualify!" he shouts, "I was a raucous fowl and deserved to die! Put me in!" But I want this book read in one or two sittings, something light in your hands that gets read. Thurber still glares about, bristling. "Why doesn't somebody help me? Hey, we've got enough guys right here, let's have a Walpurgisnacht." "There's always time for a last one," says his idol Robert Benchley, and clapping each other's shoulders they sing Thurber's favorite ditty, *Bye Bye Blackbird!*

And I must leave out Beethoven's cirrhosis, Schubert's baldness, lost teeth, early death, a serious talk about thrilling screen drunks and our old drinking hero natty Jack Norton, always mustachioed and in tails and rubberlegging between waiters, with sour amiability asking, "Gentlemen, I seem to have mislaid the barbershop, could you direct me?"

I would write a hymn to Dostoievsky for his creation in *Crime and Punishment* of the drunken clerk Marmeladov, who was a bag of vodka, gushing unstoppably, spending his every penny and sending his daughter out to whore so that he can beg her for " 'something for a hair of the dog! Hee, hee, hee!. . . . Pity! Why pity me?' wailed Marmeladov suddenly, standing up with one arm outstretched before him, veritably inspired, as if he had only been waiting for these words. 'Why pity me, you say? Yes, there's no reason to pity me! You should crucify me on a cross, and not pity me!' " One of the great drunks of fiction. Don't miss his falling to his knees in the family doorway as he shouts for his wife's forgiveness.

Deirdre Bair's biography of Samuel Beckett makes public his sieges of drunkenness, mental and psychosomatic illnesses, nervous breakdowns, harsh battles with his family, and superhuman loneliness. I won't rehearse them here, I'll say only a few words about his writing, its iron-clad despair, hopelessness and rich grey gloomlight, that community property of our graveyard years. Beckett, of course, goes straight to the grave for some of his finest passages, with bodiless voices mashing away on the past. They're usually supersensitive to eyesight, touch, voices, any voice, the words before sadness settles once more. Perhaps his voice alone is all he can bear, no, not even that, that tone in his head, of the heart tissued into mincemeat in his bowels and now gurgling, echoing faintly from his headbone with a grave sigh and bit of anxiety about his useless intestines, stone anus. NO ANALYSIS PLEASE. No quaquaqua duckquack acacacademic limedroppings. This hero is crucified but refuses to squirm on his nails, relishes infinite boredom, strives for a strip down to naked essence. The less said the better, a sigh is best, or less, a last light fading, rising, fading, the hero barebrained in the grave, lying there, a few spare words flashing their faint cold sheen in the nothingness. This is worse than "white logic." The carcass still jerking, a few last pricks and kicks, or not even that—let's get really uninvolved, the plain bare bones. Just a few raindrops, not too many, at most a pale scattering of flakes. No more than the distant clink of the stonecutter's hammer.

We have many books of endlessly solemn analysis of his silent laughter. The senselessness in analyzing Beckett is that his works have no stable meaning even for him (—"they revolt me"). There's no lasting point that won't shift before evening, despite patches of sacred amazement, or return to his spiritual vaudeville that is more flatfooted than funny. No Irish writer seemingly has less sentimentality or deeper gloom. His is a universe of dumb hearts, dim wits, dripping spirits, and slugs inching toward eternity on a softly-charged landscape, with tiny glimpses of the martyr's reward breaking through in pinpoint flarings. I find it boring, wonderful, inspiring, poetic, funny, abysmal—and a passionate sentimentalization so deep in stoical self-pity that, at times, surrender is impossible. When that humor is missing, out goes humanity and the tone dies away into meatgrinding. I like Beckett best when he likes himself.

Great writing about alcohol is an ocean without shoreline and I have a thick notebook of excerpts from world literature to attest to it, a sheaf of quotations to help me keep sober. One of the most stirring recoveries from excessive drinking was made by Dr. Samuel Johnson two centuries ago. W. Jackson Bate's *Samuel Johnson* tells us that Mrs. Johnson (as reported by a friend) "was always drunk & reading Romances in her Bed, where She killed herself by taking Opium." Johnson himself loved Bishop, a punch made of port, roasted oranges and sugar. The list of his illnesses, from birth forward, includes blindness in one eye, myopia in the other, partial deafness, a lifelong blackness and despair that sometimes paralyzed movement and speech, and so much illness compacted into one body that it defies belief. Here was a man who deserved to drink, but took on mountainous tasks instead, compiling a dictionary, editing the complete works of Shakespeare, writing the complete contents of a couple of magazines for several years, turning out reams of copy as a law reporter on the doings of Parliament, writing three volumes on *The Lives of the English Poets*, a novel, and on and on, as well as exercising a genius for writing poetry. It would seem that heaven itself dropped illnesses upon him to equal what it expected of him. And yet, when body and mind at last demanded it, he gave up alcohol in middle life. In my notebook I find the following from Boswell's *Life of Johnson* (Oxford University Press, 1970):

JOHNSON. I used to slink home, when I had drunk too much (p. 1022).

* * *

BOSWELL. I said, drinking wine was a pleasure that I was unwilling to give up.
JOHNSON. Why, Sir, (said he), there is no doubt that not to drink wine is a great deduction from life; but it may be necessary (p. 851).

* * *

Finding him still persevering in his abstinence from wine, I ventured to speak to him of it.—JOHNSON. Sir, I have no objection to a man's drinking wine, if he can do it in moderation. I found myself apt to go to excess in it, and therefore, after having been for some time without it, on account of illness, I thought it better not to return to it. Every man is to judge for himself, according to the effects which he experiences . . . (p. 687).

* * *

Talking of drinking wine, he said, I did not leave off wine because I could not bear it; I have drunk three bottles of port without being the worse for it. University College has witnessed this.

BOSWELL. Why then, Sir, did you leave it off? JOHNSON. Why, Sir, because it is so much better for a man to be sure that he is never to be intoxicated, never to lose the power over himself. I shall not begin to drink wine again, till I grow old, and want it.

BOSWELL. I think, Sir, you once said to me, that not to drink wine was a great deduction from life. JOHNSON. It is a diminution of pleasure, to be sure; but I do not say a diminution of happiness. There is more happiness in being rational (p. 911).

* * *

Talking of man's resolving to deny himself the use of wine . . . he said . . . I now no more think of drinking wine, than a horse does. The wine upon the table is no more for me, than for the dog that is under the table (p. 915).

* * *

We talked of drinking wine. JOHNSON. I require wine, only when I am alone. I have then often wished for it, and often taken it. SPOTTISWOODE. What, by way of a companion, Sir? JOHNSON. To get rid of myself, to send myself away. Wine gives great pleasure; and every pleasure is of itself good. It is a good, unless counterbalanced by evil. A man may have a strong reason not to drink wine; and that may be greater than the pleasure. Wine makes a man better pleased with himself. I do not say that it makes him more pleasing to others. Sometimes it does. But the danger is, that while a man grows better pleased with himself, he may be growing less pleasing to others. Wine gives a man nothing. It neither gives him knowledge nor wit; it only animates a man, and enables him to bring out what a dread of the company has repressed. It only puts in motion what has been locked up in frost . . .

SPOTTISWOOD. So, Sir, wine is the key which opens a box; but this box may be full or empty. JOHNSON. Nay, Sir, conversation is the key: wine is a pick-lock, which forces open the box and injures it. A man should cultivate his mind so as to have that confidence and readiness without wine, which wine gives. BOSWELL. The great difficulty of resisting wine is from benevolence. For instance, a good worthy man asks you to taste his wine, which he has had twenty years in his cellar. JOHNSON. Sir, all this notion about benevolence arises from a man's imaging himself to be of more importance to others than he really is. They don't care a farthing whether he drinks wine or not. SIR JOSHUA REYNOLDS. Yes, they do for the time. JOHNSON. For the time!—If they care this minute, they forget it the next. And as for the good worthy man; how do you know he is good and worthy? No good and worthy man will insist upon another man's drinking wine. As to the wine twenty years in the cellar,—of ten men, three say this, merely because they must say something;—three are telling a lie, when they say they have had the wine twenty years;—three would rather save the wine;—one, perhaps, cares. I allow it is something to please one's company: and people are always pleased with those who partake pleasure with them. But after a man has brought himself to relinquish the great personal pleasure which arises from drinking wine, any other consideration is a trifle . . . (B)ut we must do justice to wine; we must allow it the power it possesses. To make a man pleased with himself is a very great thing . . .

I [Boswell] was at this time myself a water-drinker, upon trial, by Johnson's recommendation. JOHNSON. Boswell is a bolder combatant than Sir Joshua: he argues for wine without the help of wine; but Sir Joshua with it. SIR JOSHUA REYNOLDS. But to please one's company is a strong motive. JOHNSON. (who, from drinking only water, supposed every body who drank wine to be elevated,) I won't argue any more with you, Sir. You are too far gone. SIR JOSHUA. I should have thought so indeed, Sir, had I made such a speech as you have now done. JOHNSON. (drawing himself in, and, I really thought blushing,) Nay, don't be angry. I did not mean to offend you. SIR JOSHUA. At first the taste of wine was disagreeable to me; but I brought myself to drink it, that I might be like other people. The pleasure of drinking wine is so connected with pleasing your company, that altogether there is something of social goodness in it. JOHNSON. Sir, this is only saying the same thing over again. SIR JOSHUA. No, this is new. JOHNSON. You put it in new words, but it is an old thought. This is one of the disadvantages of wine. It makes a man mistake words for thoughts. BOSWELL. I think it is a new thought; at least, it is in a new *attitude*. JOHNSON. Nay, Sir, it is only in a new coat; or an old coat with a new facing. (Then laughing heartily,) It is the old dog in a new doublet . . .

I [Boswell] mentioned a nobleman, who I believed was really unhappy if his company would not drink hard. JOHNSON. That is from having had people about him whom he has been accustomed to command. BOSWELL. Supposing I should be *tête-a-tête* with him at table. JOHNSON. Sir, there is no reason for your drinking with *him*, than his being sober with *you*. BOSWELL. Why, that is true; for it would do him less hurt to be sober, than it would do me to get drunk. JOHNSON. Yes, Sir; and from what I have heard of him, one would not wish to sacrifice himself to such a man. If he must always have somebody to drink with him, he should buy a slave, and then he would be sure to have it. They who submit to drink as another pleases, make themselves his slaves. BOSWELL. But, Sir, you will surely make allowance for the duty of hospitality. A gentleman who loves drinking, comes to visit me. JOHNSON. Sir, a man knows whom he visits; he comes to the table of a sober man (pp. 974-977).

Sobriety with an edge of steel! I may never be in the company of many writers I revere by dint of my writing, but I am body and soul in Johnson's company by virtue of abstinence. You know, reader, that he is *talking to himself* in those arguments and that he has thought and lived them through a thousand times—pure experience.

Robert Lowell was a friend. He was headed for a Nobel prize when he died. The full story of his alcoholism and mental breakdowns awaits his biographer. He was self-admittedly not sane and less so when drinking. Many of his poems witness the catastrophes he brought upon himself by enriching madness with alcohol. The novelist Marguerite Young and Dr. N. D. M. Hirsch, author of *Genius and Creative Intelligence*, both knew Lowell during his student days in Nashville and told me in private talks that he was mad even then, quite apart from alcohol. Lowell himself tells of his mother's talk with Carl Jung in Zurich: "If your son is as you have described him, he is an incurable schizophrenic." There's a weight to carry. It's possible that he might never have had a crackup and hospitalization if he'd abstained from drinking. At least he'd have avoided the drunk farm. I suspect that what was powerful in his poetry was written coming out of hangovers or while dry. He did not have to be drunk to capture the remorse in his lines about sitting up alone at night on Antabuse (a pill for treating hardened alcoholics) with the liquor shops closing around town, while he's alone with iced white wine and beer in the refrigerator but afraid that one sip will set off the Antabuse and kill him, as it can do. One sip, he thinks, would be death, and for only a moment's joy. This situation makes him feel . . . unwanted, the theme of a wonderful poem from *Day by Day*, his last book, in which, later, he thinks about hell, and that horrible moment when someone—who?—will take the wristwatch from his corpse's wrist.

He misses the booze, the sweet frenzy, he thinks it's the very breath of poetry. But then sees himself rotting on booze, trying to divide the minutes of a party so that the booze will stretch, but it's ending, the party is ending, while he stands swaying with a half-filled glass in each hand, feeling a kinship with Hart Crane, the great alcoholic poet who jumped into the Caribbean in his early thirties, and drunk though Lowell is he feels unique and subject to the hard, loving wind of poetry which the others cannot hear. This man cursed with angelic sensibilities must rot for his art, and lose until there's nothing left to lose.

We soon find him hospitalized once more, and drying out. He wonders how long he can go on breaking, this may repeat once too often. But nobody understands (despite decades of

155

poetry he's written about himself) that he cannot be allowed happiness—it is not his subject as poet, happiness is wrong for him. His third wife thinks he deliberately deserts her by getting sick—how can he tell her it's nothing personal, only poetry? His doctor compliments him on being a model patient, welcomes him back anytime, says the place suits him and admires the poet's strength. But the poet complains to himself that everybody feels he went mad because he wasn't happy with his young new wife, in fact that he was supersensitively unhappy, saw too much, felt too much, has a skin-layer missing. He sits back in the eloquent emptiness of the sanitarium, sees the date on the unread morning paper, gets the fidgets, walks about imagining a talk with the devil, thinks he may be worse than the devil, wishes he could pray to die, and doesn't expect to be alive six months from now. By poem's end, you've had a trip through the mind of a hospitalized poet, as he longs for home but wonders if the sanitarium itself isn't home. Or perhaps his real home is madness.

In earlier poems and books he renders alcoholic despair marvelously, it is the color of the mop and water in the grey galvanized bucket. He sits drunk, his eye fixed on the cheese wilting in the rat-trap, the milk hardening in the cornflakes bowl, the shining horror of car keys and razor blades in an ashtray. His second wife thinks he might kill her, then get sober, he's such a screwball. He's still thinking of razors, has a jackhammer anger about himself. He's so unjust, monotonous, and mean. Her only thought is how to keep alive when he swaggers home at five in the morning, whiskey-blind, and lusting for one last elephant-screw in the sack. What woe he brings to marriage! He's such a supersensible soap bubble. She lies awake with ten dollars and a car key tied to her thigh, trying to fathom what makes him tick. He's not blind, he goes on recording his faults, making poetry out of madness and with a clear eye watching the crimes his hand is up to. But his spirit is ill. He sobs in every cell. His hand is at his throat. His mind is not right. I myself am hell, he tells us, and nobody's here. . .

156

I sat in on his poetry seminar at The New School and through the years attended his readings. These were very emotional and vague and audiences responded with great applause while Lowell drank up the full throb with a satyr smile. His newer poems would go over my head, but after a few years they'd swell with fervor or deathliness or rage. His classroom readings were slow carnage, worrying and troubling the lines, with much hair-rubbing, the poem laid bare. His tongue, in his letters to magazines, could leave an awful and majestic blister, and he once answered a play-reviewer in *The Village Voice* with a thwack that left the page tingling and the reviewer's ribs staved in. I once got a hand-written letter from his second wife Elizabeth while Lowell was away (hospitalized), her jittery or spidery hand saying that she was answering his mail during his illness: I imagined Lowell in the wards while Mrs. Lowell sat carrying on and admired her. Seven years before he died, my middle wife and I were dinner guests at his apartment during the Christmas season. Or rather uninvited guests, since we were brought along as translators for a Chilean interviewer. Robert Lowell opened the door, greying, bespectacled, skulking.

"I'm afraid Carlos misunderstood me. We didn't expect you for dinner and we really don't have enough to go around. We're just sitting down now. Perhaps you'd like to go away and come back." A baleful and majestic glare. But we were penniless (down to tokens) and the subzero blizzard winds outdoors had wilted my wife, so I launched her forward through this intimidation and we went in, shucking our coats in a vastly tall living room among tall chairs and a royal couch under a heaven-hanging balcony and ceiling-high library.

After introductions we were seated in candlelight, myself in a noble bucket of sticks beside Lowell at table's head, and Elizabeth Lowell swooped out of the kitchen with a steaming casserole of cabbage and knockwurst. It was odd, sitting without a plate, and I cozied Lowell's ashtray onto my bare corner. Lowell loomed like Beethoven beside me, a dusty bottle of Margaux rising beside his wine glass, and led the table talk. He wore an old peach-brandy-fuzz jacket, its fibers straining and rounded to his bulking back, and a candy-stripe shirt with pastel block-stripe tie—the candlelit lord from Boston. It was like finding myself seated beside Dr. Samuel Johnson, literary dictator of London. And like Boswell, I went home that night and wrote it up.

"What *is* whist?" he asks the table. "It's a kind of Tory bridge or something, isn't it? Are they still playing it? I just discovered that the stories I've been telling for years are *canards . . .* I've been telling canards!"

During this bit of lexicography I see that this party's been going on for a few hours. Laird Weary, a guest, cries out something about women and canards and Lowell replies, " 'Man does, woman is,' Graves says. Isn't that what you mean? Carlos, you can't learn anything at a writer's workshop, can you?" he asks, bullyragging.

"What?" Carlos says, aglow and desperate. "I no quite understand your question, ha ha."

"I mean, surely a poet has nothing to learn at a workshop?" Lowell says, which strikes my ear as, Why are you wasting your time at a carpenters' convention?

"There are many things I feel important about it," Carlos answers.

Lowell broods over writers' workshops with the grim smile of a lifeguard at the Flood. He asks about me and I say I write poetry and novels, but shove my poetry away out of sight. Lowell slumps into his cabbage dolefully. He perks up as Elizabeth delivers a fresh bottle of Margaux to him and a glass for me. The corkscrew arrives and he begins pouring. "Have some?" he says over my glass.

"Very little." I don't mean to drink it.

"Very little?"

"One drop is suicide."

"Oh, we have tons of it!" Lowell laughs, pouring away like Fortunato.

"You write poetry?" Elizabeth asks.

"Oh, yes. But it takes six months after writing prose to get your head saturated again for poetry. And then you can't write prose because you're over-condensing all the lines—they take forever!"

"You can't do them both together, Don!" Lowell laughs, his great hand falling avuncularly on my shoulder while he eats. He may live as a conservative aristocrat but his hair has a new Beethovenian backmat.

Lowell and Laird Weary are nettling reputations and Laird's clowning brings out a trace of boorishness in Lowell. Lowell asks Carlos if he's met an older, bull-tongued poet of the soil during his travels. "He's a sort of scratchy poet," he says. "Wouldn't you say he was *scratchy*?"

"No, I don't know," Carlos says. "When I first meet him in Texas, he was very heavy drinking. So I cannot tell too much about him."

"He writes better drunk," Lowell says. "—but still *scratchy*."

After this amusement, American poets are measured against their thin-talented British counterparts so that the American poets are not criticked directly. Discussing unsung college poets, Lowell grimaces like a weight lifter with very sore gums about to make a fifty-pound press with his jaw.

"Some mute inglorious birds!" Laird Weary cries over his glass.

"The trouble is they're not mute enough," Lowell says, "they *write* endlessly!" I see armadas of midnight poems sailing to oblivion across the plains of the Republic. Poets without Lowell's magic germ-plasm, as when his pen dips down into subconscious inks for his elegy on Roethke:

> *helpless elemental creature.*
> *The black stump of your hand*
> *just touched the waters under the earth,*
> *and left them quickened with your name. . . .*

So when he comments on poets this evening, I know he measures by God-given standards of aristocratic germ-plasm.

"When I was reading with Parra down in Venezuela, I asked him what he thought was the difference between German and Anglo-Saxon, and he said, 'Manure!' "

"*What* did Parra say?" Carlos asks.

"He said, 'Manure!' " Lowell says down the knackwurst. "You know there's not really much difference between German and Anglo-Saxon, the stock words are from the same roots." This suggestion is mauled over by Laird Weary, despite Lowell's status as a linguist. "Parra said, 'When I think of Anglo-Saxon, I feel that my hands and my nose are full of soft, swarmy, smelly ordure! German is not rich quite this way.' " Lowell crumbles manure over his plate, then sinks hungrily into the small of his chair, grinning. "Parra understands language as gesture! *I see the first Angle landing on Britain's shore and* clubbing *the first Celt he meets—*" Lowell's fist rises over his plate "—and when the Angle finally has the Celt down, split-skulled and bowels spilling, the Angle cries, 'Hah! You language, me gesture!' "

Laird Weary roars over his brass grenadier's mustache, an unseen flagon of Rhenish down his face. "*HO! HO! HO!*"

Lowell glows into the turmoil of his cabbage. His mouth flies kind, gallant flags that suddenly droop as the damned Sisyphean rock begins to roll back over him. He keeps a stammer under flattening pressure and, too self-respecting for a cliché, hulks like a suffering buffalo over every verb. His voice is ardently tense and deep tenor. He strives, wherever he is, to be worthy of his work, and of the gnarled ghosts of his New England ancestors ("What are we in the hands of the great God?" he asks in "Mr. Edwards and the Spider").

Carlos asks what he thinks of a certain Neruda translator.

"His ear is a ball of dough with old razor blades in it."

His wife delivers more wine. Lowell burns with a smile. "I said X.X. has an ear like a ball of dough with old razor blades in it, darling."

"I've never heard that before."

Down the table I watch a guest who has said nothing all evening. Checkered-vest dandy, he looks like Edgar Allan Baudelaire, that shared bowl-shaped skull and spitting eye. He eats nothing, never even lifting his fork, but wets his small, spiteful lower lip constantly and nervously at his wine glass, not drinking, only inhaling whatever fumes arise from his lip. When Lowell laughs, he turns his bulbous forehead toward Lowell, the better to vent his pity on Lowell's pain. The greater Lowell's laugh, the more burnt the guest's eyes are. These guests, this dinner, this olympian gnattering, his eye says, is not patrician and not even Bostonian but only an exhalation of wine fumes. His hands are tiny, as if dispossessed of all power for work, the fingers almost boneless. Lowell's fingers, roped over his fork or pinching his wine stem, are massive, swollen with work. The odd guest, for all his dissimilarity, responds to Lowell's humor with the almost chemical familiarity of a blood-joined brother.

Lowell asks, "Carlos, do you know Randall Jarrell?"

"Randall . . . Ja . . . *Jarrell!* Ah, yes! I hear of him this afternoon."

"He was our best critic and wrote our best war poetry."

"He is dead, no?"

"I thought you might want him on your list."

"My list, it is contemporary. I have on my list . . ." Carlos runs through his list of deadbeat wordwhirlers he hopes to interview: I writhe for Lowell but Lowell takes the list deadpan. "What do you think of them?"

Lowells cuts out a maverick academy poet, speaks well of him and warns, "But catch him when he's sober. Now Jarrell, he was so enthusiastic, and a great quoter. You wanted to read whatever he was writing about. That's the mark of a great critic—enthusiasm."

Laird Weary's young wife tells my wife Jackie that she's writing a thesis in library science. "I'm tracing the influence of William Morris, the Pre-Raphaelite poet and craftsman, on

American bookmaking. His *poetry* isn't read today."

"But his chairs still stand up?" asks E. A. Baudelaire, unheard.

Mrs. Weary tells Jackie, "It's our sixth wedding anniversary. We were married in front of that very fireplace in the living room."

"Ees your anniversary!" Carlos rises, gallant as a Chilean poet-cultural planner, circles the table and kisses her raised cheek. His glasses butter with second thoughts. "That ees what we do in Chile on anniversary," he says in mock-epic and is cheered.

"Interpret! Interpret!" Laird Weary cries at me, blue eyes robotic.

I feel oblivion.

Carlos' wife Mathilde says in Spanish, "Laird reminds me of Octavio."

"Interpreter!" Laird Weary cries. "What the hell are you here for?"

Mathilde says, "I say you remind me of our friend Octavio in Santiago who ees great lover."

Laird Weary kisses her hair, his hand on her leatherette bell-bottom thigh. She laughs. "Yes, that ees Octavio!"

Laird Weary's hand drops from her thigh to an eight-week pure-brown Burmese. "It's the cat! the cat! The cat is a leather freak!"

Lowell, facing the distant living room, points, "Look! my laurels are fading." He nods toward a life-size, smooth white-marble bust of a boyman on the living-room table: a wreath of russet laurel crowns the bust. "Those laurels were given to me on my fiftieth birthday. Now they've turned brown."

"Ees that you?" Mathilde asks, staring at the bust.

"No, that's Richard Wilbur."

Laird Weary roars, flagging down the wine.

As I join myself in a cigarette, E. A. Baudelaire's glance enters my eye like graphite. My wife smiles from her bare, polished, plateless corner two candle flames away. E. A.

Baudelaire's twisted lip assures me that all is vanity at the best of parties, for the uninvited guests as well as the celebrants.

Lowell looks at him. "When did Shakespeare retire? Forty-six? I'm fifty-one. . . ."

"How would you like to have written *Hamlet* at thirty-six and *Lear* at forty-one?" E. A. Baudelaire leads Lowell on. "And thirty-four other five-act verse plays in sixteen years? Which is impossible. . . ."

"Of course Middleton's hand is obvious," Lowell says. "But Shakespeare wrote the greater body of his work in a ten-year period. From about thirty-six to forty-five or so. He had run down by *The Tempest*. *The Tempest* is a disaster, don't you think? It only has about two hundred good lines." Lowell digs up the good passages for E. A. Baudelaire. "Peter Brook wanted me to tinker with it for a new production—" he holds up the play like a seashell necklace "—do away with that masque and the most boring parts. Nothing happens during the masque! It just shouldn't be there."

"Oh, but it should," E. A. Baudelaire says mildly. "The whole play is one thought in the mind of Prospero, one drop of water like *A Midsummer Night's Dream*. All the colors and hues keep changing so that everyone sees everything differently, with a different tawniness or green or blue, and the masque is the great moment of clarified light before Prospero pulls the clouds back over it."

"That's very interesting, I'd never thought of that."

"The masque is the reason he wrote the play."

"Well, I knew it was impossible. I couldn't rewrite *The Tempest*, heaven knows. My God, I haven't. . . ." He shudders, disclaiming such immodesty. "We know how he wrote. I mean, he must have written like lightning, the pages blotchy and black, then gone back and filled in." (I think back and see the perfectionist winepages cranked from Drunkspeare's Underwood. Shakespeare?—that lightning-master must have been sober.) "You have to wait for it to come and catch it when it does, it isn't always there—although it *seems* always there for him—and it's such a miracle when it does come. It was finally burning out in *The Tempest*."

"What if your best friend," E. A. Baudelaire asks Lowell, "has steeped himself in philosophical magic and written a play called *The Alchemist?* Wouldn't some of your best friend's interests rub off on you when you start out to write about a philosopher on an island? And—"

"But Jonson's *Alchemist* is such a great bore, so overwritten and dense. Of course, he wrote the best poem we have about Shakespeare, but I think Shakespeare knew where Jonson was merely pedantic."

"Ah! but what if you also had a king who literally believes in all the spirits, witches, fairies, magicians and fishman creatures you write about, and who himself has published a book called *Daemonologie* in which he describes the little magic beasties on his island that he rules? And—"

"Did Shakespeare know James that well? I mean, behind the scenes, or did he know him just at court?"

"I believe they're only mentioned being together twice. But what if—beyond living and writing on an island with a king who writes about demons—you have this king who institutes the conception of the divine right of kings and thinks that he has been touched by God and that God talks through him? Your James is so sublimely touched by God that he's lame and can't walk because he's with the Spirit. He has to be carried everywhere and the clothes practically have to be peeled off his body—I mean they are rank! Now you, William Shakespeare, have just written thirty-some plays about kings, and the qualities of aristocracy and nobility have consumed your life as a poet. So, when you have a king who, in his mind, rules not by the consent of the people, but by divine purpose, with God at his ear and speaking through his tongue as surely as He spoke through Moses and Isaiah, and who in the vulgar view might be thought a reeling idiot but who in your view might be a great deal more, then you, William Wildwords, would be *inspired*. Then you might very well create a play about a magician ruling on a small island that is written for your James the First on his island and for no lesser mortal. I don't think Shakespeare was writing for the audience by then, and what seems crotchety to Peter Brook wasn't crotchety to Shakespeare at all."

"What's this all about?" asks Laird Weary, turning from Mathilde.

"Did Shakespeare write *The Tempest* for the audience or for James the First?" Lowell says.

"Oh, that tripe! And what a place for Shakespeare to place his play—Bermuda'll never sell. James Bond, okay, he can go to Bermuda. But Shakespeare down there with all those British tourists, it's a fiasco! A play about hauling logs. . . ."

I hear invisible Ariel say, "Hey, old magickmon, whot you want next from your see-through, swift houseboy and all his abili*ties*?"

"Poof on Bermuda!" says Laird Weary.

Carlos and Mathilde listen blissfully through candlelight, the chat like cloudborne whales leaping the ceiling. Carlos shrugs at me with joy.

Elizabeth Lowell serves coffee ("It's the maid's day off!"), and bourbon-flavored chocolates signal meal's end. The party moves toward the living room. I have some blessed coffee and head instantly toward the pot for a second cup. Laird Weary refills his glass. E. A. Baudelaire leafs lazily through a new illustrated edition of Lowell imitations on the coffee table. I try the bourbon cordials.

My God, they're needled with real bourbon! My chemistry prickles. First sauce in eighteen months and it's awful: chocolate bourbon. I sit, dizzy. The juice crawls through my cells in a red haze. I reach for the pot and it's empty.

A deep breath, I can hardly walk. I go out to join the others in the living room. My head floats, cloven from my shoulders.

I am Ludwig the Mad, King of Bavaria. The Lowell ceiling rises to Wagnerian heights and tall buckets of spears stand in each corner. It is an artist's studio such as no poet in America dwells in. The balcony overhangs the living room and far up the north wall a skylight rises embedded in Lowell's psyche. The wall skylight is very high up and large as myth. Two walls rise in slabs of books, each wall fifteen shelves high and ten feet wide, and arched against each library bank rise Cyclopean traveling-ladders attached to ceiling rods along which the angled ladders roll. No bright dust jackets, the library is banked with battered, musty sets (*The Rise of the Dutch Republic* for one), worn-looking Lowellian books, old clopped covers, foundering, scuffed, grizzled *books* hunting for a man to strike down and drown in. But the Wagnerian throb filters through greying puritan patches, large grey Civil War photos, with a red velvety Pre-Raphaelite painting of two nudes for a dash of Swinburne and decadence. Here sits the whitesmooth bust of Narcissus crowned with russet. A far wall is blocked and covered like The Gotham Book Mart with small, framed photographs of family and ashen literati. Another wall holds blowups of Lowell at his readings and a group of Pasternak rarities, photos of him at twenty, bony and sensual. Here are high black-and-white line drawings by Sidney Nolan, larger than their first appearance in *The New York Review of Books*, where they accompanied Lowell's poems. Behind the couch rises a tall Christmas tree with handmade paper ornaments, while, depending from the ceiling, a knobbed, brown wooden chandelier curls and rocks like an heirloom from the *Mayflower*, lost in the air.

Laird Weary walks about with a wineglass, a captain in mufti who has wandered into a liquor ad. Elizabeth Lowell stands moaning over the record collection. "We don't have the new Beatles album! It costs twelve dollars. Well, that's too much! But we have the last two Beatles records." Instead she plays an organ-rock record and the Wagnerian twilight fills with a howling Southerner: "No place to go! Ahm fulla woe! Ah can't run! Ah can't hide! Help me, help me make it to the other side!"

Mathilde rolls her blue-beetle eyes at E. A. Baudelaire.

"Music is stronger than death," he tells her, "but not this music."

In wineglass and gown, Elizabeth Lowell chases the cat which has escaped from the kitchen and now runs over the couch. Her accent's gallumphing Kentuckian and she cries over the music like a Williams heroine, "That cat! Until a couple of hours ago I had control over that cat and I was faster than *it*. Now it's faster than me! It keeps getting out of the kitchen faster than I can close the door, I'm sorry, people. Oh, I give up."

I circle back through Lord Lowell's castle to refresh myself at his table. Some sweettoothed sonofabitch has eaten all the bourbon chocolates! Elizabeth Lowell groans by with the coffeepot into the kitchen and I follow, eye peeled for a chocolates box. The lemonyellow kitchen bangs my eyeballs and is boomerangshaped and cluttered. At the stove, Elizabeth Lowell stands overpouring boiling water from a saucepan into a dripolator and missing.

"This pot!"

She descants on coffeepots, dripolators and filter tops, grinders and coffee beans. She sweeps by me with the pot into the living room. I see no chocolates box. "Here's more coffee, everybody!" I am hungry. I plant myself first in line as she rushes off to shoo the cat from Lowell's laurels.

"You know," Mathilde tells Lowell, "I always think of you from your pictures as—"

"How? I look older than my pictures."

"Much *colder* in them."

"As like engineer!" Carlos says.

"Oh, here are some better pictures," Lowell offers, to correct their South-American impressions. He shuffles through a stuffed closet for pictures and stretches over a chair for one off the wall. Framed, himself with fingers raised as if conducting at a reading, his figure captured at a chiseled Etruscan slump at once erect and glorious, and in the other trim and Apollonian with a golden haircut. Neither suggests the baleful and noble anger in many of his published photographs.

My wife glides by on wine.

I hand him a two-record album, *Mozart's Complete Masonic Music*, a gift I've brought. "Mozart is my favorite! I've never heard this." He holds it out to his wife, pleased. "*The Marriage of Figaro* is the greatest music ever written," he says.

"By heavens," Lowell asks Carlos, "have you read da Cunha?"

"*Rebellion in the Backlands*, the Brazilian *Moby Dick*"—Elizabeth Lowell. "I've given away about a hundred copies! That dear old duck Samuel Putnam translated it in the Forties." She's an editor on *The New York Review of Books*.

"It's very much like *Moby Dick*," Lowell seconds as if funding a peace drive from the Forty-second Street Library steps. "The same pace of description of the Brazilian heartland with epic brooding about the nature of man, a narrative about an insane rebellion like Ahab's quest."

Twelve-years-old Harriet Lowell comes down from the balcony and Lowell crushes her. Through the guitar-drench Elizabeth Lowell delivers a monologue to my wife while Lowell climbs a library ladder in search of da Cunha and sits on the ceiling, wincing at us. He seems about to declaim Aeschylus to us from his Promethean pose he's holding up there. I feel very tender suddenly and hope he doesn't jump.

Harriet stands gimlet-eyed beside me where I sit. My nose twitches—a free question! "Say, what's the cat's name?" She doesn't believe I've spoken to her—I *am* something of a hairy ambush from Beyond the Electric Circus on the Lower East Side. "What?" "What's the cat's name, *heh, heh?*" "Summer." I rack my brain for Civil War memorabilia. "Oh, after Fort Summer?" She stares at me as if I were Hairshert Hammersaxon. As she goes to bed, it occurs to me I'd meant Fort Sumter. . . . I'm not getting through. My bourbonaded mind's not right.

Swim! Try the couch! I sink into the French rowboat couch

and list upward through looming guitars, Carlos, Lowell and Laird Weary above me.

Carlos, hectic yellow, "What do you say now we have questions to you we have written? On the tape recorder?" I writhe. It's futile.

Laird Weary takes his cue from Lowell while Lowell transmogrifies into a bust of Beethoven surfacing through heavy molasses and gumming a song. His pride rises, he's unable to decide, Laird Weary reflects on the crisis: We're myths, above petty data of tapes. Carlos burns, embarrassed, and over a thrombosis of drums The Doors gargle "Light My Fahr!"

Too much—Elizabeth Lowell and E. A. Baudelaire slip on a Mozart Masonic record. . . . *Wolfgang, Ludwig and Johann père awake to music in the air.* . . . Carlos shaken, at a loss about his interview, so, to help, I ask Lowell about his early connection with The Fugitives, the circle of *Southern Renascence* poet-critics at Vanderbilt and Kenyon. This circle originally met on Nashville Friday evenings at the home of a recluse linguist, Sidney Hirsch, whose work I've been studying lately.

"When you were at Kenyon, did you ever meet Sidney Hirsch?"

"I saw him once or twice. Did he ever do anything beside appear in that Vanderbilt University Press book, *Fugitives' Reunion?*" Lowell asks.

"Oh, no, he didn't write—he wouldn't. He's dead now."

"He was a mystic, wasn't he? Did you work with him?"

"No. I know his brother quite well," I say.

"Well, what *did* he do?"—Laird Weary.

"I'm hard put. He didn't do anything. Real mystics don't do anything. He was a master of languages. He taught himself Greek and Latin and a lot else and could follow a word or a thought through several tongues at once."

"Some Fugitives thought very, very highly of him," Lowell says, "but Tate and Red Warren, I think, couldn't take him very seriously."

"What do you think about him?"—Laird Weary, grimacing, my reverse in a sleeper's mirror.

"Well, he lived alone for about fifty years, and just studied, and practiced some kind of religious exercises like Kundalini Yoga. Several times a day . . . so that he was in a sort of ecstasy of languages for about fifty years."

Laird Weary mutters and turns away. He turns back. "What's your interest in this?" Is he acting out Lowell's animus?

Tongue-tied on the couch. Sidney Hirsch piques me keenly. The more I learn, the less I speak loosely. "To wake up."

He digs into himself for a word that summarizes his feelings. "And what do you plan to turn into gold out of dross metal?"

"Myself."

Laird Weary catches a goldfish in his throat. His eyes pop at me. "*Shit!*" he says.

My heart falls away, sliced by a weaver.

"You really believe this horseshit?" he asks from a great height.

My head floats and my veins flood with radiant green booze. His face spills.

"Well, I don't have to stand here and listen to your fucking shit."

I say nothing, too surprised at wounding him. He turns, huffing, and strides to the coat pile. Mrs. Lowell follows into his muttering. "What's wrong, Laird?"

"He's so full of motherfucking horseshit that I'm going home."

On the couch with me, Carlos and Mathilde sit with stunned golden smiles.

My wife stands before me, amazed and smiling. "What did you say to him?"

"Nothing."

"Did you bring up that topic?"

"No."

"I don't have to listen to that sonofabitch!" Laird says again to Lowell and his wife, who try to calm him. He's into his coat. Lowell mumbles something to him, then leaves to walk Laird home. No good-byes. Mrs. Weary and her mother left earlier, as if antennae may have picked out familiar gray waves in the air. Mozart sings, *"Brothers, surrender wholly to the bliss of your feelings!"*

"Well!" Elizabeth Lowell says in a flutter. "He drinks a lot. He's not like that. He didn't mean all that really. Did you say something to him?"

"No!" The hand-folded bluebird of innocence.

She sits in her queen-backed chair. *"What* could have got into him?"

No answer. She keeps elaborating an apology for him. Finally, "Don't mind Laird, he just had too much."

"He's passionate."

"What?"

"He's passionate."

She looks away for something else to think about. "What's your book about?"

"It's called *The Body Artist* and it's about a world-famous surgeon named da Vinci who's won two Nobel Prizes and has never lost a patient. He's a very spiritual surgeon."

"It's his *Hamlet*," Jackie says.

Elizabeth Lowell grinds away at this grainy information. Silence.

"Brando da Vinci," I say.

Her eyes drill me. "Did you say this is a novel?"

"This is a modest *Magic Mountain* and *Doctor Faustus.*"

She eyes Jackie. "You said *Hamlet.*"

Jackie nods, all happy teeth.

Lowell returns, grinning in agony. "Well, heh, heh— Laird drinks like a fish!" He sighs, sitting beside me, his great spirit muffled with flesh.

"Would you mind saying what you're working on?" I ask.

Lowell rubs his hair flat, orchestrating an answer, and suffers. It's real and I'm sorry I asked. "I'm working on a great long poem that follows the seasons of a year. It's more or less finished. I'm putting what last I can into the page proofs. I've published bits of it already." He searches intensely for the right word for each feeling on Gethsemane. He looks jellied and tinned in the phantom snowlight.

"What did you think of Mailer's descriptions of you in *Armies of the Night?* It was very funny when he had you falling back on your head and there wasn't any headrest."

"I was quite flattered! Norman really didn't have to say all that about me." Lowell smiles, his eyes ringed with good humor. He looks wine-weary. "Are the Masons still active?" he asks. "Don't you think Mozart just wrote Masonic music for ceremonies? He wasn't a high officer?" He cocks an ear. "This is so beautiful!"

E. A. Baudelaire says, "This Masonic music isn't for the opera house, it's de-Italianized, de-theatred, man-to-man, yet very elevated. All his life he was hungry for fellowship. He fell in with the Masons like an alky into A.A."

Lowell sits in momentary oblivion, a wine-dark cloud passes over him but is repressed. He launches into his memories of South America. "What's it like beyond Buenos Aires?"

"Nothing is there," Carlos says. "Is just pampas."

"Kilometers and kilometers of grass," Mathilde says.

Seas of grass fill the Lowell living room.

Lowell's voice deepens. "Well, I think 1968 will be remembered as a turbulent year of small disasters. Nothing turned out as I expected!"

The porcelain clock strikes eleven. We're ready to leave. But Lowell turns to Mathilde and Carlos beside him on the couch and abruptly jumps into poetry and memories of poets, deadpanning as the old virtuoso and national poet. For his Latin visitors, it is the full sonata. Lowell rubs his hairline back until his forehead bulks like Beethoven's, his hair matted and falling. He weaves themes and fragments from everywhere on his keyboard into a ten-minute monologue. His voice just scrapes his cords and issues in a sulky whisper, completely inner, as if he has closed the lid to muffle his pianissimo. Admiration creeps over me. Here is the germ-plasm itself. My wife, lost, shakes her head at me. Carlos melts limpidly as Lowell's sonorities gently rake him. Mathilde sits erect and burningeyed. Lowell, kindly grim mouth compelling us to his mood, lecturing blue eyes swelling his glasses, weaves on. "And once you met the force in the green fuse that drove him, you were aware of his attractive genius . . ." Carlos blazes eagerly. ". . . Of course, those seeds on the sill after the burial are so great, you know it's genius . . ." Carlos nods profoundly. ". . . he was so alive and fresh. I knew him. If you were in the same room with Dylan Thomas you gravitated toward him. I did. He was a great performer. *Actor,* really. If you heard him declaim a poem once, you knew you'd hear it four more times that night. He mostly read other poets aloud, only about one poem in nine was his at a reading—he really was modest about himself. He had about ten great poems—of course, he was a minor poet—he took one rhetorical quality of Yeats's and blew it up and used it better than Yeats (he admired Yeats profoundly) but he became the narrower poet for it—really minor. His best poems were about five, with another five shifting and changing as his second best five. His best writing was really his short stories, every phrase brimming and fresh, so alive. He's the only one who did anything with prose. Of course he couldn't hold an audience or penetrate it as completely as Frost or Eliot, and he really wasn't as good a poet as Auden or Pound or perhaps even Graves. But he really *was* better than Swinburne. . . ."

Mathilde sits like a toothpaste ad, reacting. She has never heard of Swinburne.

Lowell's memories curl off into heaven and he is silent. E. A. Baudelaire's head tilts back in sleep, his sockets scraped with peace. Silence. Time to tiptoe out.

I launch McManis, a friend I think is the greatest living poet. Lowell smiles grimly. I go on. Alarm fills Lowell's glasses. He glowers into the carpet, wishing I'd finish. I hear myself raving but can't stop.

"Oh, you really do think he's good?"

I nod happily. "—and of course no one's ever heard of McManis!"

"Of course not!" Lowell chuckles, sighing.

"I'll leave you a bunch for your files. Look 'em over sometime."

"Well, I can't fail to do that!" Lowell says, accepting my McManis bouquet.

We rise to leave. Lowell is full of warmth, soberly charming, his handshake large and masculine. "I love those Mozart records."

"Watch out for the hidden symbols."

"I was afraid of that," he says into the rug.

"You may find yourself wanting to join the Masons."

On the street Carlos releases his exhilaration. "But you know that last ten minutes on the couch, I don't understand five words! Just the 'force through the green fuse.' His talk was like James Joyce. It was difficult, no?" he asks Mathilde.

"I only sit and smile," she says. "But his voice—"

"*Ahhh!*" Carlos signs, his head severed, "—Ecstasy! Nothing do I understand what he says, but that voice is so moving I know he is a very deep man and become convinced he is great poet. Just by his voice! I never have experience like that. Such deep feeling! Like the softest cello, like music, like Beethoven, no?"

Whenever I heard of Lowell after this evening he was just going in or coming out of a hospital and getting ready to couch more of his disasters in free verse. His more public poems had rhyme and meter. He was a highminded, private man, a Boston aristocrat who enjoyed the mortification of getting shitfaced and writing about it. He was puffed up with humiliation. Self-abasement was his meat and drink, and his last years

174

were a banquet of it as his last books make plain, with poems quoting Elizabeth's agonized letters to him about his new marriage. Self-abasement seemed to awake his most vital senses. His writing, of course, shows a dry hand. There is nothing slovenly about his verse. He could bring springlike freshness to suffering, a shocking brightness to his self-recognition, moral force to self-loathing. Of this kingly man we can say, he was every inch a drunk—a grim Marmeladov on his knees in the family doorway. He died in a taxi coming from Kennedy International into Manhattan, of heart failure. A man with enormous power over language and early formal discipline, a gripping speaker who brought electric doom to his best and his worst lines, a charmer who could show you his forebears with loving vigor, his Navy father in the bathtub, his mother's body wrapped in tinfoil and being shipped home from Italy for burial, a man highborn, educated by the finest teachers, friend to distinguished philosophers and connoisseurs, intimate with the most celebrated writers, composers and poets of his time, himself magnificently well-read and distinguished in languages, a scholar-poet when he wished, who dared to imitate the gods of ancient and modern tongues and English them, whose own tongue could leave welts on his critics, rend them with slow carnage, stave their ribs in (you feared him), a loving father, spellbinding teacher and lecturer, acclaimed playwright, a large-boned, robust, tall, commanding man, his every word authentic, rooted in the past, deep-spirited, a poet loved and honored, the Nobel Prize at his fingertips, to be all that and casually, knowingly, relentlessly, to step aside from himself, that man not the real man, only a supersensitive bubble of a man, the real man rising from wine, grand, his feelings slowly inflating, Caligula appearing, the tyrant of unhappiness, or satyr with a racing ego, brain humid, no longer hamstrung and straining, but smirking and baleful, bullyragging, brooding, grim, slumping, doleful, translating some patch of Horace or Catullus in the back of his mind while listening or talking, his big fatherly hand falling on your shoulder from the heavens of fame, grinning, joking, glowing through some veiled turmoil, a kind, gallant smile suddenly clamped, keeping a stammer under flattening pressure, hulking now, then tensely ardent, striving to be worthy of his work, burning, his eye spitting fire, something writhing within him, his ropelike fingers clenching, his face swelling, then deadpan, boorish, worn-looking, foundering, halved, salvaged by a deep breath, then hammered, jagged, smashed, fat, suffering, scuffy, razored, savage, dynamited, torn, lolling, spilled, cracked, numb, grizzled, sunken, ashen, huddled, burned out, groveling, dragged back, trembling, hopped up, suffocating, hunting, lunging, drowning. Where is our Pulitzer Apollo with the golden haircut, firebreathing and twenty-seven, his gimlet eyes aerial, puckish, blinking?

Trusting in his recuperative powers like an elephant's. And then the power died. A man laid bare and spreadeagled, every inch a drunk.

Who took the wristwatch from his wrist?

July 4, 1980
Greenwich Village—
The Tower, Cape Cod